The Canadian Spelling Program 2.1

2

Ruth Scott
Sharon Siamon

gage EDUCATIONAL PUBLISHING COMPANY
A DIVISION OF CANADA PUBLISHING CORPORATION
Vancouver·Calgary·Toronto·London·Halifax

Canadian Cataloguing in Publication Data

Scott, Ruth, 1949-
The Canadian spelling program 2.1, 2
Rev. ed.
ISBN 0-7715-1590-1

1. Spellers. 2. English language - Orthography and spelling - Problems, exercises, etc. I. Siamon, Sharon. II. Title.
PE1145.2.S34 1997   428.1   C96-931859-6

Editor: Kim Blakey
Design: Pronk&Associates
Illustration: Dayle Dodwell, Joanne FitzGerald,
          Loris Lesynski, Jackie Snider
Cover Illustration: Jackie Snider

Acknowledgments
The publisher acknowledges the important contribution of Dr. Ves Thomas to *The Canadian Spelling Program* series, in particular the research and development of a uniquely Canadian word list as outlined in his work, *Teaching Spelling,* Second Edition (Gage 1979).

The authors and publisher also acknowledge the contributions of the following educators to *The Canadian Spelling Program 2.1:*

Lynn Archer
Surrey, British Columbia

Sylvia Arnold
Aurora, Ontario

Halina Bartley
Peterborough, Ontario

Carol Chandler
Halifax, Nova Scotia

Jean Hoeft
Calgary, Alberta

Lynda Hollowell
North York, Ontario

Caroline Lutyk
Burlington, Ontario

Judith MacManus
Riverview, New Brunswick

Denis Maika
Mississauga, Ontario

Alyson McLelland
Scarborough, Ontario

Bill Nimigon
North York, Ontario

Gordon Williamson
Winnipeg, Manitoba

ISBN 0-7715-**1590-1**
  4 5 6 FP 01 00 99 98
Written, printed, and bound in Canada..

Contents

How to Study Your Words

You will already know how to spell some of the words in this book, but there might be some words that are hard for you.

When you need to study a word, use these steps:

1. **Look** at the word, letter by letter, from beginning to end.

2. **Say** the word to yourself and listen carefully to the sounds.

3. **Cover** the word.

4. **Write** the word.

5. **Check** the spelling, letter by letter, with the word in the list.

If you make a mistake, notice where it is. Did you make a mistake at the beginning of the word, in the middle, or at the end?

Now do all the steps over again with the same word.

1

Short **a**
c**a**t

a
one
at
cat
an
ran
can
two
man
as

See the Words

Look at each word in the list.

Say the Words

1. Say each word. Listen for each sound.

    a   as   at   cat   an   ran

    can   man   one   two

2. Say the words. Listen for the vowel sounds.

cat   hat   man

What letter spells the short vowel sound **a**
as in **hat**?

✓ Precheck

**Check your work.
Write the words
you misspelled.**

★ Powerbooster ★

When we say the short vowel sound **a** as in **apple**
or **hat**, we usually spell it with the letter **a**.

Write the Words

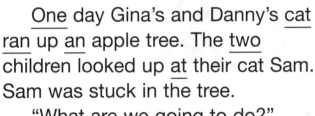

1. a) Read this story.

   One day Gina's and Danny's <u>cat</u> <u>ran</u> up <u>an</u> apple tree. The <u>two</u> children looked up at their cat Sam. Sam was stuck in the tree.

   "What are we going to do?" Danny said. Just then their uncle Nick came along. He was <u>a</u> very tall <u>man</u>.

   "<u>Can</u> you reach our cat?" asked Gina.

   Uncle Nick reached up <u>as</u> high as he could and grabbed Sam.

   "Thanks!" said Danny and Gina.

   b) Look for all the list words in the story.
   Write them in your notebook.

2. Write the four list words that begin with the short **a** as in **hat**.

3. Write the four list words that have a short **a** in the middle.

4. Write the four list words that rhyme with **pan**.

5. Write the number words that belong with these pictures.

a) <u>two</u>   b) _____   c) _____   d) _____

Word Power

1. Write the word that has the short **a** sound as in **hat**.

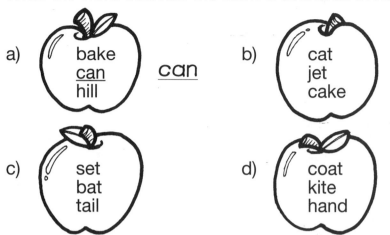

a) bake
   <u>can</u>
   hill   <u>can</u>

b) cat
   jet
   cake

c) set
   bat
   tail

d) coat
   kite
   hand

2. Fill in the blanks with the correct letter.
   Write the words.

a)

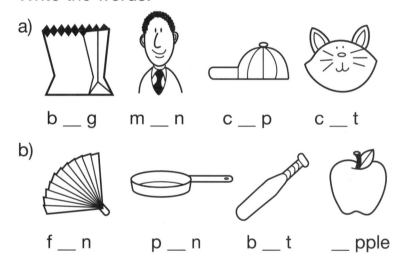

   b _ g   m _ _ n   c _ p   c _ t

b)

   f _ _ n   p _ _ n   b _ _ t   _ pple

3. Write a rhyming word to complete each verse.

a) What a funny hat

    On this little _____ !

b) Here's a man

    With a _____ .

c) The big dog sat

    On the yellow _____ .

3

SUPER
★ ★ ★ ★ ★
tag
hand
candle
flag
plan
★ ★ ★ ★ ★
WORDS

Challenges with Words

1. Write the Super Words that fit these spaces.

____ an ____

____ an

____ an ____ ____ ____

2. Solve these riddles with Super Words.
   Write the answers in your notebook.

   a) I give you light.
      When it's dark at night.
      I am a _____ .

   b) Sometimes I am red and white.
      I wave in the wind.
      I am a _____ .

   c) You run to play this game.
      It is called _____ .

Lots of words rhyme with **tag**. Try **b** and **w** to start.

3. Write all the words you can think of that rhyme with **flag** and **tag**.

4. Unscramble the Super Word on each candle.
   Write the words.

d n a c e l

n l a p

g t a

a g l f

h d a n

5. a) Write a sentence about what these children
are doing in the park.

The children are _____
_____.

b) What do you like to do in the park? Write a
sentence of your own. Read it to a partner.

6. Here are some words for things you do in a park.
Write the words that fit each shape.

a) I love to play in the ⬚⬚⬚⬚ .

b) I ⬚⬚⬚⬚⬚⬚ in the water.

c) I don't like ⬚⬚⬚⬚ in my food!

Kids WORDS

sand
splash
ants

2 Short i
him

is
in
it
and
him
if
sad
big
hit
had

See the Words

Look at each word in the list.

Say the Words

1. Say each word. Listen for each sound.

    is   in   it   if   hit

    him   big   and   sad   had

2. Say the words. Listen for the vowel sounds.

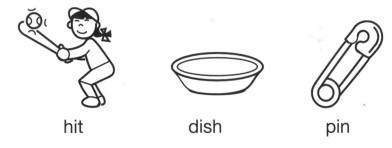

    hit   dish   pin

What letter spells the short **i** sound as in **it**?

✓ Precheck

Check your work. What words do you need to study?

★ Powerbooster ★

When we say the short vowel sound **i** as in **it** or **pig**, we usually spell it with the letter **i**.

6

Write the Words

1. a) Read this story.

> Danny <u>is</u> going to visit his grandmother and grandfather <u>in</u> the <u>big</u> city. He takes a bus <u>and</u> his grandparents meet <u>him</u> at the station. Later they play baseball. Danny can <u>hit</u> the ball very well. Too bad his grandfather can't catch!
>
> Danny is <u>sad</u> when <u>it</u> is time to go home, but he has <u>had</u> a good visit. "I will come back next Saturday <u>if</u> I can," he says.

b) Look for all the list words in the story. Write them in your notebook.

2. Write the four list words that begin with the short vowel **i** as in **it**.

3. Write the three list words that have the short vowel **i** as in **it** in the middle.

4. Write the list words with the short vowel **a** as in **cat**.

5. Write the pairs of list words that fit these boxes.

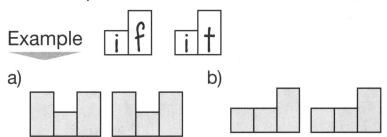

Word Power

1. Write a list word that rhymes with each of these words.

   pin   dig   sit   bad

2. Write these sentences in your notebook.
   Fill in the blanks with list words.

   a) I gave h _ m a book to read.

   b) Maria h _ t the ball over the wall.

   c) _ f you come back, I will be happy.

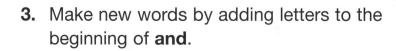

3. Make new words by adding letters to the beginning of **and**.

   b __and__   l _____

   h _____   st _____

   s _____   gr _____

4. a) This clown bounces off his bike to make us laugh.
   Write about some other ways clowns make us laugh.

   b) Draw or paint a happy or sad clown face.

Clowns _____
_____
_____
_____
_____
_____.

8

SUPER

★ ★ ★ ★ ★

mitten
wings
sand
litter
insect

★ ★ ★ ★ ★

WORDS

Challenges with Words

1. Write the Super Words that fit these boxes.

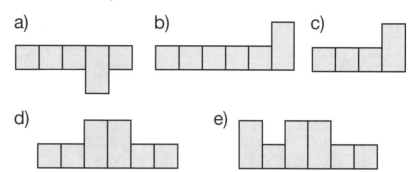

a)

b)

c)

d)

e)

2. Answer the questions under this picture with Super Words. Write the words in your notebook.

Put litter here.

a) What is in the basket? _____

b) What is flying over the basket? _____

c) What does it use to fly? _____

d) What is under the basket? _____

e) What is in the dog's mouth? _____

3. Write your own sentences to tell what will happen in the picture.

4. Use the clues to write the Super Words.

a) a word with two **t**'s and rhymes with **kitten** _____

b) a word with two **t**'s and rhymes with **bitter** _____

c) two words with the small word **in** in them

_____ _____

5. Make a chart like the one below. Fill in the chart with all the insects you know. Draw some insects to go with your chart.

Insects that fly	Insects that crawl	Insects that bite or sting

6. Imagine that one morning you wake up and you have wings! Write a story about where your wings came from and what you will do with them.

3

Short e
pet

went
pet
bed
get
let
saw
red
book
good
jet

See the Words

Look at each word in the list.

Say the Words

1. Say each word. Listen for each sound.

pet   get   let   jet   bed

red   went   saw   book   good

2. Say the words. Listen for the vowel sounds.

bed   jet   pen

What letter spells the short **e** sound as in **let**?

✓ Precheck

Check your work. Underline the parts of the words you need to study.

★ Powerbooster ★

When we say the short vowel sound **e** as in **jet**, we usually spell it with the letter **e**.

Write the Words

1. a) Read this story.

> When Gina <u>went</u> to <u>bed</u>, she had a dream. The dream was about all the things she would like to have someday. In her dream, Gina <u>saw</u> a <u>good</u> <u>book</u>, a <u>red</u> toy <u>jet</u>, and a wonderful new <u>pet</u>.
>
> What kind of pet do you think Gina's parents will <u>let</u> her <u>get</u>?

b) Look for all the list words in the story. Write them in your notebook.

2. Write the four list words that rhyme with **met**.

3. Write the list words that fit these boxes.

a) 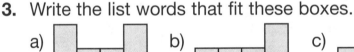 b) c)

4. Complete these rhymes with list words. Write the verses in your notebook.

a) I love to look
At a g_ _d b_ _k.

b) We found a cent,
So off we _____ .

c) My mother said
It's time for _____ .

Rhyming words don't always look the same.   said   bed

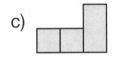
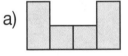
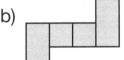
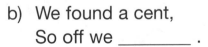
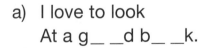
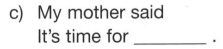

12

Word Power

1. Make words using the word wheel.
   Write them in your notebook.

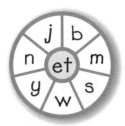

Example

jet

2. Use the pictures and list words to write these sentences.

   a) I  a r_d  .

   b) We have a  for a p_t.

   c) Nina w_ _t to  .

3. Write the list words that answer these riddles.

   a) I'm a dog or cat.   b) I am made of paper.
      I need care and love.   I have many words.
      I am a _____ .   I am a _____ .

4. a) Write about three things you would ask for if someone gave you three wishes.

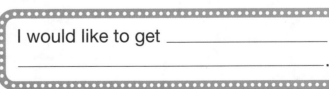

   I would like to get _____

   _____ .

   b) Draw pictures of the things you might wish for.

SUPER
★ ★ ★ ★ ★
cookie
bedroom
nest
penny
petal
★ ★ ★ ★ ★
WORDS

Challenges with Words

1. Complete the Super Words on each petal of the flower. Write them in your notebook.

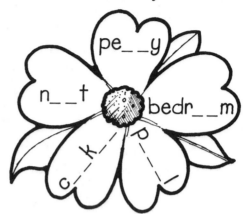

2. Find a Super Word that goes with each set of words. Write the words in your notebook.

Example	apple	orange	banana

a) bird   egg   _____
b) dime   nickel   _____
c) leaf   stem   _____
d) cake   candy   _____
e) kitchen   bathroom   _____

3. Find the Super Words that fit each of the boxes. Write them in your notebook.

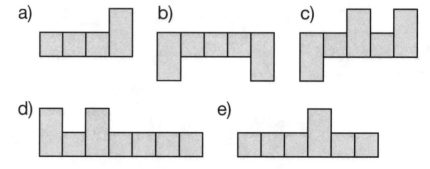

window
closet
rug
dresser
pillow
blanket
toy bin
curtains

4. Draw a picture of a bedroom. Label the different things in your picture. Some words you might need are in the word box.

5. Make words by adding letters to **est**. Write the words in your notebook.

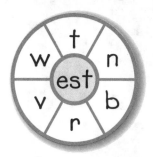

6. a) Write about how you think Inez spent two dollars at the store. What would you get?

b) Write and draw a picture about how you would spend two dollars. Read your story and show your picture to a partner.

7. Write the words that fit the sentences.

a) A _____ is another word for a dollar.

b) A _____ is another word for a penny.

c) We _____ a loonie and got back one cent!

Kids
WORDS

cent
loonie
spent

4 Short o
dog

dog
on
of
got
fell
help
hot
lot
yes
not

See the Words

Look at all the words in the list.

Say the Words

1. Say each word. Listen for each sound.

on   of   dog   got   lot

hot   not   fell   help   yes

2. Say the words. Listen for the vowel sounds.

dog

mop

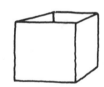

box

What letter spells the short **o** sound as in **hot**?

✅ Precheck

Check your work. Write the words you misspelled.

★ Powerbooster ★

When we say the short vowel sound **o** as in **hot** or **dog**, we usually spell it with the letter **o**.

Write the Words

1. a) Read this story.

One <u>hot</u> day Danny and his <u>dog</u> Max went to the park. Danny went too high <u>on</u> the swing. He <u>fell</u> and hit the ground with a big BUMP. When Danny <u>got</u> up, his foot hurt a <u>lot</u>. He could <u>not</u> walk.

"Go for <u>help</u>, Max," cried Danny. Max ran out <u>of</u> the park. Soon Danny's father came running up.

"Max came and got me," he said. "Are you hurt?"

"<u>Yes</u>," said Danny, "but Max saved me."

b) Look for all the list words in the story. Write them in your notebook.

2. Write the four list words that rhyme with **pot**.

3. Write the list word that means the opposite of **no**.

4. Write the three list words that have the short vowel **e** as in **let**.

5. Write the list words that fit the boxes.

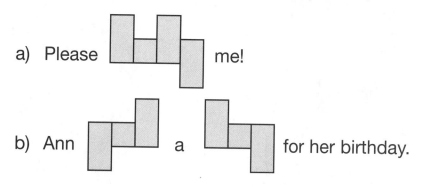

a) Please ⬚⬚⬚ me!

b) Ann ⬚⬚ a ⬚⬚ for her birthday.

Word Power

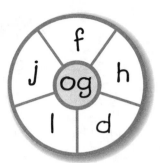

1. Use the word wheel to write words that end with **og**.

2. Solve the riddles. The answers all rhyme with **fell**. Write the answers in your notebook.

   a) I ring when school begins. _____

   b) I am the opposite of buy. _____

   c) If something is a secret, you should never do this. _____

   d) I am a place to get water. _____

3. Unscramble the list words on the dog.

Let's see
– help rake the lawn
– help wash the car
– help make lunch

4. Make a list of three things you can do to help at home. Read your list to a partner.

Help in the house	Help outside
_____	_____
_____	_____
_____	_____

SUPER
★ ★ ★ ★ ★
helpful
doghouse
onto
pocket
bottle
★ ★ ★ ★ ★
WORDS

Challenges with Words

1. Use the clues to write the Super Word that fits in each pocket.

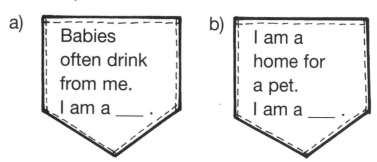

a)
Babies often drink from me. I am a ___ .

b)
I am a home for a pet. I am a ___ .

2. **Doghouse** is a word that has two short words in it. We call this a **compound word**.

Match the words in column A with the words in column B to make compound words. Write them in your notebook.

A	B
cup	ball
milk	corn
meat	cake
pop	shake

_____
_____
_____
_____

3. Complete the Super Words below the bottles. Write the words.

_ _lp_ _l   _o_ _l_   p_ _k_t

4. Write a sentence with each word from exercise 3.

19

5. Write the Super Words that fit the boxes.

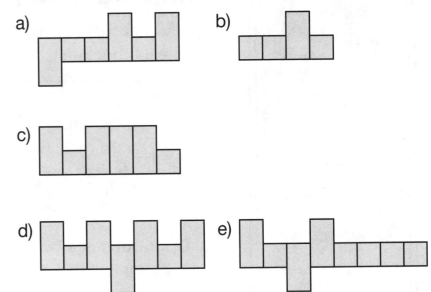

a)

b)

c)

d)

e)

6. Write new words by changing vowels in the words below.

a) Change the **o** in **pocket** to an **a**.

b) Change the **o** in **pocket** to an **i**.

c) Change the **o** in **bottle** to an **a**.

d) Change the **o** in **onto** to an **i**.

7. Fill in the blanks with the new words from exercise 6. Write the sentences.

a) The firefighters won the _____ against the fire.

b) Mario has a small _____ of cookies.

c) He put his hand _____ his pocket.

d) We have a white _____ fence.

8. Pretend there is a new student in your class. List ways that you can be helpful to your new classmate. Read your list to a partner.

5

Short i   Short o
six   box

Word List
will
did
six
lost
box
doll
off
from
because
new

See the Words

Look at the shape of each word in the list.

Say the Words

1. Say each word. Listen for each sound.

   will   did   six   off   doll

   box   lost   because   from   new

2. Say the words. Listen for the vowel sounds.

   ship   fish   pin

What letter spells the short **i** as in **it**?

3. Say the words. Listen for the vowel sounds.

   lost   doll   box

What letter spells the short **o** as in **hot**?

✓ Precheck

Check your work. Underline the parts of the words you need to study.

★ Powerbooster ★

We usually write short **i** with the letter **i** and short **o** with the letter **o**.

Write the Words

1. a) Read this story.

> When Gina was <u>six</u> years old, she <u>lost</u> her toy dog, Bingo. Gina was sad <u>because</u> Bingo was her favourite toy. She liked Bingo better than a <u>doll</u>.
>
> Then one day Gina's grandmother came to visit. "What's the matter, Gina?" she asked.
>
> "I still miss Bingo," said Gina.
>
> The next day Gina found a <u>box</u> in her room. She took <u>off</u> the lid and there was a <u>new</u> dog just like Bingo! It was a present <u>from</u> Grandma. "Thank you, Grandma. I <u>will</u> take good care of this toy dog." Gina said. And she <u>did</u>.

b) Look for all the list words in the story.
Write them in your notebook.

2. Write the three list words with the short vowel **i**.

3. Write the four list words with the short vowel **o**.

4. Write the list word that fits the sentence.
Shanti was happy <u>b</u> _ <u>c</u> _ _ _ _ she hit a home run.

5. Find the list words that fit the boxes.
Write each word.

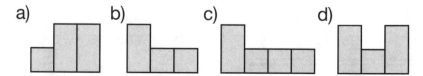

a)　　　　b)　　　　c)　　　　d)

Word Power

1. Two words rhyme in each box. Write the pairs of rhyming words.

a)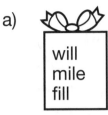

will
mile
fill

b)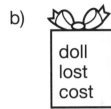

doll
lost
cost

c)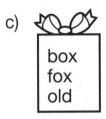

box
fox
old

2. Write the words that belong with these pictures.

a) _four_ _hats_

b) _____ _____

c) _____ _____

d) _____ _____

3. Fill in the blanks with list words.
Write the sentences.

a) The d_ _ l fell o_ _ the table.

b) D_ _ you get a letter f_ _ _ Susan?

4. a) Use each pair of words to write a sentence.

new   lost   will   because

b) Paint or draw a picture to go with your sentences.

SUPER
★ ★ ★ ★ ★

sixty
news
dollar
kick
middle

★ ★ ★ ★ ★
WORDS

Challenges with Words

1. Be a word detective. Write the Super Words that fit these clues.

   a) two words with double consonants
   b) three words with short **i**
   c) one word with short **o**
   d) one word with a different meaning if you take the **s** off the end

2. Write sentences with each of the Super Words.

3. **New** and **news** have different meanings. Fill in the blanks in these sentences with **new** or **news**.

   a) John's _____ bike is black and yellow.

   b) We watched the _____ on TV.

   c) Our house isn't _____ . It's fifteen years old.

   d) I have some good _____ for you!

4. Use the letters **o** and **i** in the corners of the box and any of the other letters to make words. You can use the letters more than once. Write as many words as you can.

I found sixteen words!

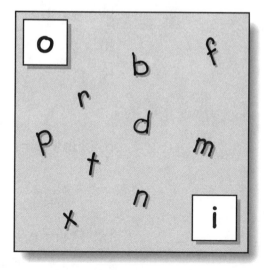

o

b   f

r

d

P   m

t

n

x   i

5. Write your words from exercise 4 in two columns in your notebook.

Words with short **i**	Words with short **o**
dip	not

6. a) Add letters from each box to **ick**. Write the words in your notebook.

Example   **fl** + **ick** = flick

 st   k   sl   tr   qu   + _____ **ick**

b) Think of other letters you can use with **ick**. Write the words.

7. Write the class news of the day. Be sure to put the date at the beginning.

_____ day, _____ _____

Today, _____

_____ .

8. Write the words that fit the boxes in this story.

My dad gives me a big ⬚⬚ when

I ⬚⬚⬚ all the toys in my toy box. Then I

clean up all the ⬚⬚⬚ .

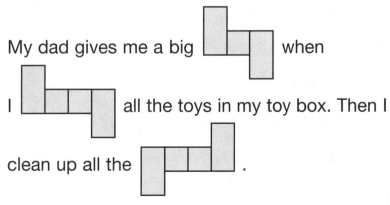

25

6

look

say

cover

write

check

Looking Back

Here is a list of words from Units 1–5 that may be hard for you.

one	from	lost	good
went	off	of	new
because	saw	help	him

1. Study the words using the five Study Steps.

2. Say each picture word. Write the word and put a circle around the vowel.

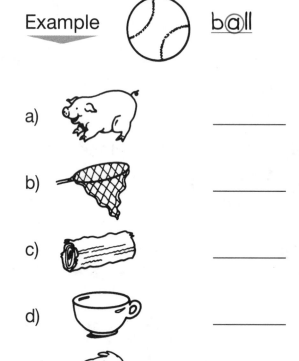

Example   b(a)ll

a) _____

b) _____

c) _____

d) _____

e) _____

f) _____

3. Write the number word that belongs with each picture.

a)

b)

c)

4. Look at the words on each kite.
Write the words that rhyme.

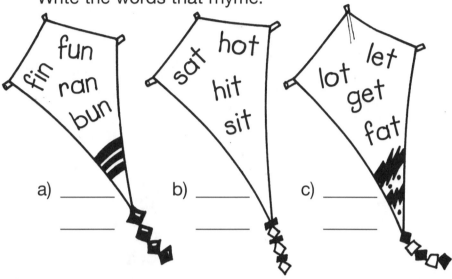

fun
fin
ran
bun

hot
sat
hit
sit

let
lot
get
fat

a) _____

b) _____

c) _____

_____

_____

_____

5. Use the letters in the corner of each box and any of the other letters to make words. You can use each of the letters more than once. Write as many words as you can.

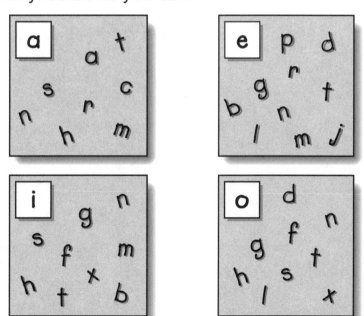

a   t
a
s   c
n   r
h   m

e   p   d
r
b g   t
n
l   m j

i   n
g
s
f   m
h   x
t   b

o   d
n
g f
t
h s
l   x

6. a) Divide your page into four columns like this.

short **a** as in h**a**t	short **e** as in b**e**d	short **i** as in h**i**ll	short **o** as in d**o**ll
cat			

b) Say each word in the box below. Write the words in the correct column in your chart.

cat	tent	will	him	went
pet	plan	sat	off	box
red	big	frog	got	had
saw	hit	with	fin	six
and	dot	lost	hand	help
bend	jet	man	cost	fog

7. Make your own review list. Add words you like, special classroom words, or words you misspelled on the Unit Tests.

Don't forget!

Look   Say   Cover   Write   Check

Think of your own special ways to study review words.

28

Fun in the Playground

tag

catch

baseball

run

throw

slide

bat

skipping

hang

rope

climb

swing

monkey bars

1. All the words in this picture tell about things you do in the playground. Make a class list of playground words to use in your writing.

Things I see	Thing I hear	Things I do

2. Work with a partner. Write five safety rules for the playground. Use the pictures and words from the top of the page to help you.

Example   Don't run up the slide.

This is a capital.

This is my house.

Grammar Games

Sentences

What is a sentence?

A sentence has **words**.

A sentence has a **capital** letter at the beginning.

A sentence has a special mark at the end.
Usually, this mark is a **period**.

1. Write these sentences in order.

a) | brother | My | pizza. | loves |

b) | girl | The | over | jumped | rope. | the |

c) | my | house. | Here | is |

I am a period.

2. Answer these questions.
The answers have been started for you.

a) What is your name?

My name is _____ .

b) Where do you live?

I live in _____ .

c) What games do you like to play?

I like to play _____ .

Dictionary Games

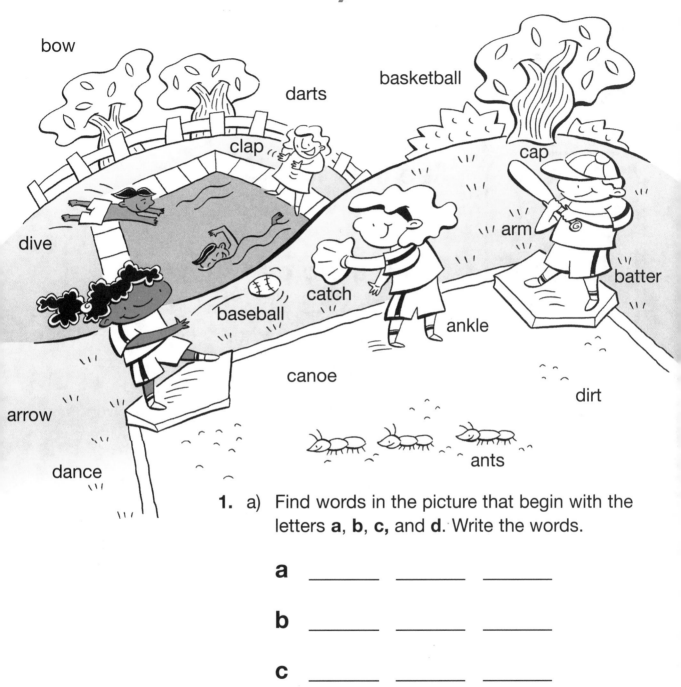

bow
darts
basketball
clap
cap
dive
arm
catch
baseball
ankle
batter
canoe
dirt
arrow
ants
dance

1. a) Find words in the picture that begin with the letters **a**, **b**, **c,** and **d**. Write the words.

   a _____ _____ _____

   b _____ _____ _____

   c _____ _____ _____

   d _____ _____ _____

   b) Write sentences using some of the words you found.

7

Short **u**

c**u**p

fun
up
us
fast
run
jump
am
cup
sun
next

See the Words

Look at each word in the list.

Say the Words

1. Say the words. Listen carefully for each sound.

up us jump fun cup

run sun fast am next

2. Say the words. Listen for the vowel sounds.

run   jump   sun

What letter spells the short **u** as in **cup**?

3. Say the words. Listen for the short vowel sound **u** at the beginning.

up   us

What letter makes that vowel sound?

✓ Precheck

Check your work. What words do you need to study?

★ Powerbooster ★

When we say the short vowel sound **u** as in **run**, we usually spell it with the letter **u**.

Write the Words

1. a) Read these lines.

> I leap from the oven
> I <u>jump</u> <u>up</u> from the pan
> I dash through the door
> As <u>fast</u> as I can.
>
> <u>Next</u> I dance in the <u>sun</u>
> I jump up and down
> I <u>run</u> down the street
> I run through the town.
>
> I have lots of <u>fun</u>
> Can you <u>guess</u> who I <u>am</u>?
> You can't catch me
> I'm the Gingerbread Man.

b) Look for all the list words in the poem. Write them in your notebook.

c) Write the two list words that are not in the poem.   _s   c_p

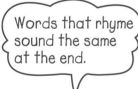

Words that rhyme sound the same at the end.

2. Write two list words that rhyme with **fun**.

3. Write the list word that has the short **e** sound as in **let**.

4. Find the list words that fit the boxes. Write each sentence.

a) The Gingerbread Man ran  .

b) I like to ⬚⬚⬚ in the water.

Word Power

1. Use the letters on the bees to write words with the short **u** sound as in **cup**. You can use each letter more than once.

2. Write the math words that fit the blanks.

Here are your math words.
subtract
plus
sum

a) 5 + 5   The _____ is ten.

b) 5 – 3   You _____ three from five.

c) 4 + 5   Four _____ five equals nine.

3. Write the opposite of each word.

a) big ___small___

b) up _____

c) fast _____

4. Fill in the first four blanks with list words. Fill in the next two blanks with your own words. Write the whole poem.

I get _____ with the _____ .

I _____  out to play.

I _____ in the _____ .

I _____ all day.

SUPER

★ ★ ★ ★ ★

sunshine
upstairs
breakfast
jumping
runny

★ ★ ★ ★ ★

WORDS

Challenges with Words

1. Write each Super Word to match the pictures.

a) _____

b) _____

c) _____

d) _____

2. Write about the breakfast foods you like.
Write about what dinosaurs, giants, and space
creatures might like for breakfast.

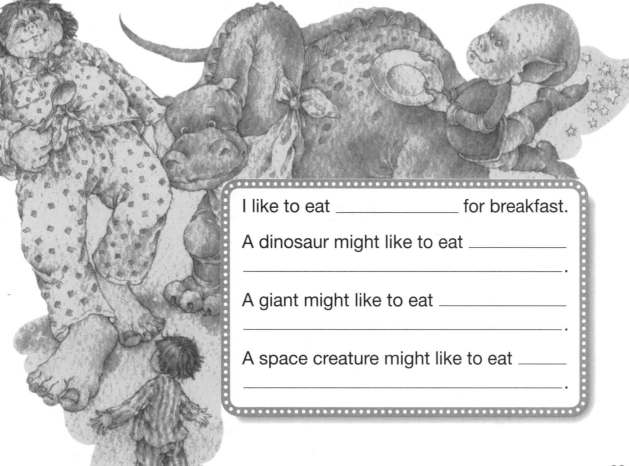

I like to eat _____ for breakfast.

A dinosaur might like to eat _____
_____.

A giant might like to eat _____
_____.

A space creature might like to eat _____
_____.

3. Unscramble the Super Words to complete the sentences. Write the sentences.

a) What do you have for **rafstekba**?

b) I like **unshnies** better than rain.

c) Anita likes **ngimpuj** in puddles.

d) We have six rooms **pstrauis**.

e) This pudding is too **yurnn**.

4. Fill in the blanks with words that rhyme with **runny**. Write the words.

a) The clown is _____ .

b) A little rabbit is called a _____ .

c) A bright and warm day is _____ .

5. Look at the picture. Write a story about the children in the picture. You might need some words like the ones below.

teeter-totter   afraid   heavy   exciting

Kids
WORDS

munch
crunchy
bubble gum

6. Unscramble the words in these sentences.

a) I like to **cmhun** on an apple.

b) I can blow a big bubble with **ubeblb umg**.

c) That cereal is **yccrhun**.

8 Vowels with r
ar
c**ar**

car
upon
pig
park
start
but
just
bus
farm
bad

See the Words

Look at each word in the list.

Say the Words

1. Say each word. Listen for each sound.

car   park   farm   start   upon

but   bus   just   pig   bad

2. Say each word. Listen for the sound at the end.

car   bar   jar

What letters spell the **ar** sound as in **far**?

3. Say each word. Listen for the **ar** sound in the middle.

farm   park   start

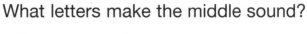

What letters make the middle sound?

★ **Powerbooster** ★

When we say the sound **ar** as in **car**, we usually

spell it with the letters **ar**.

Write the Words

1. a) Read this story.

The Lost Pig

Once <u>upon</u> a time a farmer had a little <u>pig</u>. One day it ran away. Soon the pig came to a <u>park</u> with many beautiful flowers. "I'll eat those flowers," said the pig. <u>But</u> before it could <u>start</u>, a big dog chased it far down the road. "I'm having a <u>bad</u> day," said the pig. "I wish I could take a <u>bus</u> back to my <u>farm</u>." <u>Just</u> then, a <u>car</u> came along. It was the farmer, and he took his tired pig home.

b) Look for the list words in the story.
Write them in your notebook.

2. Write the four list words with the sound **ar** as in **far**.

3. Write the four list words with the short **u** as in **cup**.

4. a) Write the list word with the short **a** as in **hat**.

b) Write the list word with the short **i** as in **it**.

36

Word Power

1. Write a list word that rhymes with the word on each star.

bar · dart · bark · harm

2. Make new words by adding letters to the beginning of **ark** and **art**.

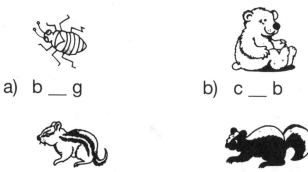

ark

a) p _____

b) d _____

c) b _____

d) m _____

art

a) p _____

b) t _____

c) d _____

d) st _____

3. Fill in the missing letter in the animal names below. Write the words.

a) b __ g

b) c __ b

c) chipm __ nk

d) sk __ nk

4. Many stories begin with **Once upon a time.** Write a story about an animal. Start your story with **Once upon a time.**

SUPER
★ ★ ★ ★ ★

butter
parka
arm
piglet
carpet

★ ★ ★ ★ ★
WORDS

Challenges with Words

1. Read these riddles. Write the missing Super Words in your notebook.

   a) It's warm and soft.
       It has a hood.
       It's worn in the winter.
       It is a _____ .

   b) It covers the floor.
       It can be any colour.
       It keeps your feet warm.
       It is a _____ .

2. Write two more riddles with Super Words and words from your Personal Word List.

3. Make two short sentences into one long sentence.

   Example

   | The boys play in the park. | The girls play in the park. |

   The boys **and** girls play in the park.

   a) I like bread. I like butter.

       _____ and _____ .

   b) Your pants are dusty. Your hands are dusty.

       _____ and _____ .

   c) I hurt my arm. I hurt my hand.

       _____ and _____ .

4. a) Copy this chart in your notebook.

Mother	Baby

b) Match the mothers and babies in the list below. Write them in your chart.

Mothers dog cow goose cat sow mare

Babies calf kitten piglet puppy colt gosling

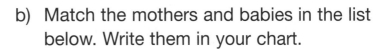

Our **ar** words

carpet
jar
_____
_____
_____

5. Look for words in your books and charts that have **ar** in them. Make a class list or add them to your Personal Word List.

6. a) Write a story about a toy or robot that has a special arm that can do many things.

b) Design an ad for your robot. Share it with a partner.

9

Long o
g**o**

Long e
m**e**

I
we
me
go
so
be
no
white
blue
he

See the Words

Look at each word in the list.

Say the Words

1. Say each word. Listen for each sound.

   go   so   no   we   me
   be   he   I   white   blue

2. Say the words. Listen for the vowel sounds.

me

we

   What letter spells the long **e** as in **me**?

3. Say the words. Listen for the vowel sounds.

   go   no   so

   What letter spells the long **o** as in **go**?

✓ Precheck

Check your work. What words do you need to study?

★ Powerbooster ★

The letter **o** spells the long **o** in words like **go**.

The letter **e** spells the long **e** in words like **me**.

40

Write the Words

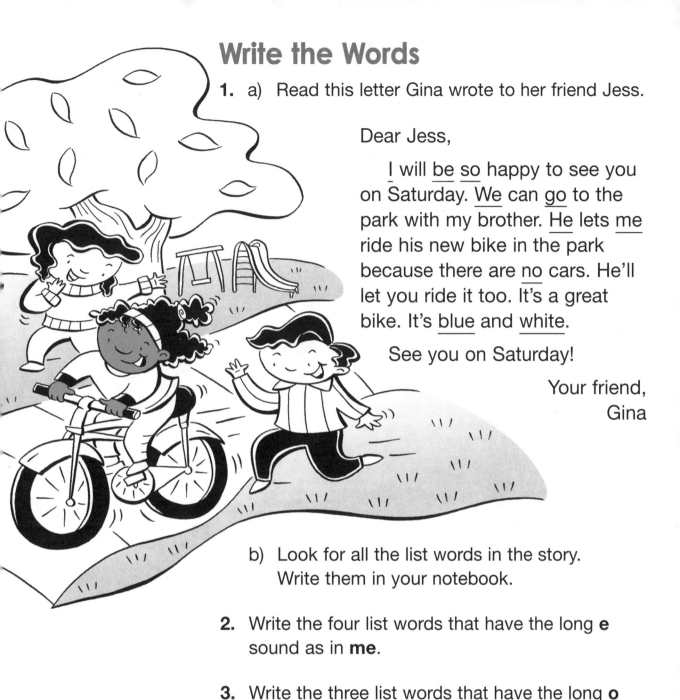

1. a) Read this letter Gina wrote to her friend Jess.

Dear Jess,

   I will <u>be</u> <u>so</u> happy to see you on Saturday. <u>We</u> can <u>go</u> to the park with my brother. <u>He</u> lets <u>me</u> ride his new bike in the park because there are <u>no</u> cars. He'll let you ride it too. It's a great bike. It's <u>blue</u> and <u>white</u>.

   See you on Saturday!

Your friend,
Gina

b) Look for all the list words in the story. Write them in your notebook.

2. Write the four list words that have the long **e** sound as in **me**.

3. Write the three list words that have the long **o** sound as in **open**.

4. Write the list word that rhymes with **glue**.

5. Write the list words that fit the boxes.

a) b)

Word Power

1. Write this story in your notebook. Fill in the blanks with these list words.

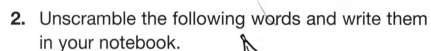

   I   he   go   I   we   so

   Asim and _____ live on the same street.

   _____ play together and _____ to the

   same school. _____ am _____ glad

   _____ is my friend.

Hint! They all rhyme with **white**.

2. Unscramble the following words and write them in your notebook.

   a) iekt   _____

   b) tibe   _____

   c) eriwt   _____

_____day, _____

Dear _____,

Can you come _____

_____ ?

We will _____

_____.

    Your friend,

    _____

3. Write the colour list words that fit the blanks.

   a) The sky is _____ .

   b) Snow is _____ .

4. Write a letter to someone you like. Tell them what you will do to have fun at your house when they come to visit you.

SUPER
★ ★ ★ ★ ★
beside
between
nobody
write
glue
★ ★ ★ ★ ★
WORDS

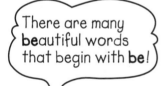

There are many **be**autiful words that begin with **be**!

Challenges with Words

1. Be a word detective. Write the Super Words that match these clues.

   a) a word that has two silent letters

   b) a word that means the opposite of somebody

   c) two words that have long **e** spelled **e**

2. Look at each picture. Write the missing word in each sentence. Use these words.

   behind   between   before   below   beside

   a) The dog is
       _____ the cats.

   b) The number 2 is
       _____ the number 4.

   c) The bat is
       _____ the ball.

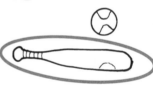

   d) The sun is
       _____ the clouds.

   e) Simon put his cup
       _____ his plate.

3. Solve this riddle. Write the answer.

If I started with **b**, I would be blue,
But my colour is white,
And I rhyme with **you**!
What am I? _____

.

I   see   trees.

4. Write these picture sentences in words.

a)  the tween the .

b) Do **U** want **2** go **B4** lunch?

5. Fill in the missing letters to write a Super Word.

_o_ody

6. Write **Me** at the top of the page. Draw a picture of yourself and write words or sentences underneath that tell about you.

Me

My name is _____ .

I am _____

_____ .

I like _____ .

Kids WORDS

Mars
Venus
Pluto

7. All the Kids Words are names of planets. Fill in the missing letters in the words below.

a) M __ __ s is sometimes called the red planet.

b) P __ __ __ o is a planet that is far from the sun.

c) V __ __ __ s is a planet that is covered with thick clouds.

10

Long **a**
c**a**k**e**

walk
name
work
came
has
take
make
have
cake
made

See the Words

Look at each word in the list.

Say the Words

1. Say each word. Listen for each sound.

   make   cake   take   came   name

   made   has   have   walk   work

2. Say the words. Listen for the vowel sounds.

   cake   lake   plate

What letters spell the long **a** sound as in **cake**?

✓ Precheck

Check your work. Underline the parts of the words you need to study.

★ Powerbooster ★

The long **a** sound is often spelled with the letters

a__e as in **name** and **cake**.

Write the Words

1. a) Read this story.

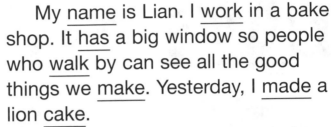

My <u>name</u> is Lian. I <u>work</u> in a bake shop. It <u>has</u> a big window so people who <u>walk</u> by can see all the good things we <u>make</u>. Yesterday, I <u>made</u> a lion <u>cake</u>.

As soon as I put it in the window a man <u>came</u> in. He said, "That lion looks so real I can hear it roar. I'll <u>take</u> it home to my family and we'll <u>have</u> it tonight."

b) Look for the list words in the story. Write them in your notebook.

Can you find a silent letter in **talk**?

2. Write three list words that rhyme with **rake**.

3. Write the list word that rhymes with **talk**.

4. Write two list words that have the short **a** sound as in **hat**.

5. Write the list words that fit the boxes.

a) Will you 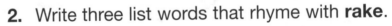 home with me?

b) We 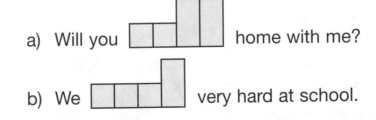 very hard at school.

46

Word Power

1. Write the list words that fit the blanks.

   walk   make   work   take

   a) I _____ in a pet store.

   b) You _____ good cookies.

   c) We _____ to school every day.

   d) I _____ my toys to my bedroom.

2. Write the list words to complete these rhymes.

   a) I am happy you came.
      What is your n _ _ _ ?

   b) We wanted to talk,
      so we went for a w _ _ _ .

   c) I wish you would make
      a big chocolate c _ _ _ .

3. Make four new words with each word wheel.
   Write the words.

  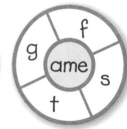

4. a) What do you like to make? Write three
      sentences using this pattern.

   I like to make _____.

   b) Write a story about something you tried to
      make in the kitchen. Read your story to a
      partner.

SUPER
★ ★ ★ ★ ★
sidewalk
homework
handmade
cupcake
snowflake
★ ★ ★ ★ ★
WORDS

Challenges with Words

1. Each Super Word is made up of two short words. These are called **compound words**. Write each one.

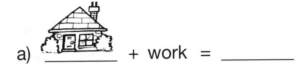

a) _____ + work = _____

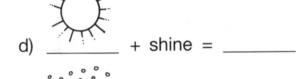

b) _____ + cake = _____

c) _____ + made = _____

d) _____ + shine = _____

e) _____ + flake = _____

2. Find the Super Words that fit the boxes. Write them in your notebook.

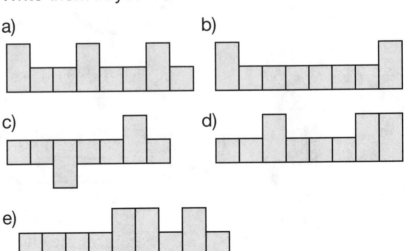

a)

b)

c)

d)

e)

3. Write a sentence with each Super Word.

4. Write the compound word for each picture. All the words are about sports.

a) _____

b) _____

c) _____

d) _____

5. a) Write about your favourite sport. Try to use some compound words in your sentences.

My favourite sport is _____.

I love it because _____.

b) Read your sentences with a partner. Suggest changes to each other's writing.

11

Long e
b**ee**

see
gave
three
seven
green
tree
ate
funny
bee
baby

See the Words

Look at each word in the list.

Say the Words

1. Say each word. Listen for each sound.

   bee   see   tree   three   green

   gave   ate   baby   seven   funny

2. Say the words. Listen for the vowel sounds.

tree   bee   three

What letters spell the long **e** as in **see**?

✓ **Precheck**

Check your work. Write the words you misspelled.

★ **Powerbooster** ★

In some words the long vowel sound **e** as in **bee** is spelled with the letters **ee**.

Write the Words

1. a) Read this story.

Last week Danny went to a pet shop. In the window he could <u>see</u> <u>seven</u> <u>baby</u> rabbits and <u>three</u> kittens. <u>Danny</u> got a little white rabbit and took it home. He put it in a box under a big <u>tree</u>. He <u>gave</u> it lots of <u>green</u> leaves. The rabbit <u>ate</u> everything. It even tried to eat a <u>bee</u> that landed on its nose!

"You <u>funny</u> bunny," said Danny.

b) Look for the list words in the story. Write them in your notebook.

2. Write the picture words that have the long **e** as in **see**.

3. Write the three list words with the long **a** sound as in **age**. Underline the two words that have long **a** spelled with the letters **a_e**.

4. Write the two list words that you find in a math book.

Word Power

1. Write the list words that fit the boxes.

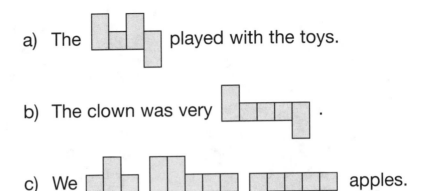

   a) The [boxes] played with the toys.

   b) The clown was very [boxes] .

   c) We [boxes] [boxes] [boxes] apples.

2. All of the picture words below have long **e** spelled **ee**. Write the words in your notebook.

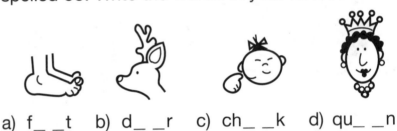

   a) f_ _t   b) d_ _r   c) ch_ _k   d) qu_ _n

3. Read the riddle. Write the missing word in your notebook.

   My name is a letter
   That rhymes with tree.
   I make honey
   Because I'm a _____.

4. a) Write sentences using the pairs of words below.

   baby   funny   gave   seven

   b) Paint or draw a picture to go with one of your your sentences.

SUPER

free
parade
seventeen
eleven
sunny

WORDS

Challenges with Words

1. A hungry mouse is eating these Super Words. Write the words in your notebook before it eats all of them.

a) para _de te_

b) seven _ _ _ _

c) sun _ _

d) _ _ _ _ ven

e) f _ _ _

2. Write a Super Word that goes with each set of words below.

a) clowns, balloon _____

b) hot, summer _____

c) nine, ten _____

d) nineteen, eighteen _____

3. The words in this tree all have the long **e** sound spelled **ee**. Write three sentences using some of these words. Read your sentences to a partner.

heel keep need
greedy beetle meet peel seed
deep feel feet chimpanzee seem seen
beef geese week weed
feed knee

ee

I saw two _____
last _____.

I have never _____
such big _____.

Please don't _____
the _____.

53

Sunny must be the first word. I'll circle the **s** because it's the letter of my hidden word.

4. Use the letters of the word **seventeen**. Write as many small words as you can.

5. Rewrite the scrambled Super Words.

a) ◯ _ _ _ _   nyusn

b) _ ◯ _ _ _ _   leevne

c) _ _ ◯ _   rfee

d) ◯ _ _ _ _ _ _ _ _   vtennseee

e) ◯ _ _ _ _ _   arpaed

Use the circled letters to write a hidden word to fit the blank in the following sentence.

My kitten likes to _____ in my boot.

6. Make a list of three things you like to do on a sunny day in summer. Make a list of three things you like to do on a sunny day in winter.

On Sunny Summer Days I Like To:	On Sunny Winter Days I Like To:

7. Write the words that fit the boxes in this story.

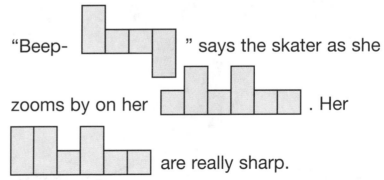

"Beep-⬚⬚⬚" says the skater as she zooms by on her ⬚⬚⬚⬚⬚⬚. Her ⬚⬚⬚⬚⬚⬚ are really sharp.

12

Looking Back

Here is a list of words from Units 7–11 that may be hard for you.

white	walk	baby	upon	ate	take
blue	work	next	start	just	funny

STUDY STEPS

look

say

cover

write

check

1. Study the words using the five Study Steps.

2. Write the picture words.

a)   d _ g   b _ d   d _ _ t

 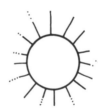 

b) p _ _ k   s _ n   p _ g

c)   t _ n   s _ _ _ k   h _ t

d) d _ sh   b _ g   n _ t

3. Write three words that rhyme with each of these words.

make   three   ate   gave

4. Write sentences with these review words.

just   upon   walk

5. Make three columns in your notebook.

long **o**	long **e**	long **a**

a) In column 1 write all the words from the box with the long **o** sound as in  .

b) In column 2 write all the words from the box with the long **e** sound as in 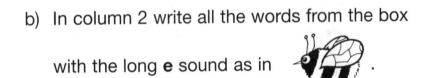 .

c) In column 3 write all the words from the box with the long **a** sound as in .

I'm going to write some of these words on my chart.

we	made	three	so	take
sad	no	tap	seven	next
make	me	cake	gave	fast
go	pet	he	baby	get
on	help	tree	see	bee
green	bone	name	mad	ate

6. Look at your review words. Write a word that matches each clue.
   a) begin _____
   b) a very young child _____
   c) move your feet _____
   d) not play _____

7. Write the first letter in each of these words to find a secret message.

> happy owls like it down at your school
> apples red eat
> cats on my igloo new gum

8. Change these words by adding an **r** after the **a**. Write the new words.

Example   pat   part

cat _____   ban _____

chat _____   ham _____

9. Make your own review list. Use words from your Personal Word List, Super Words, and words from the Unit Tests.

Get a partner to dictate your list to you.

Animals in Winter

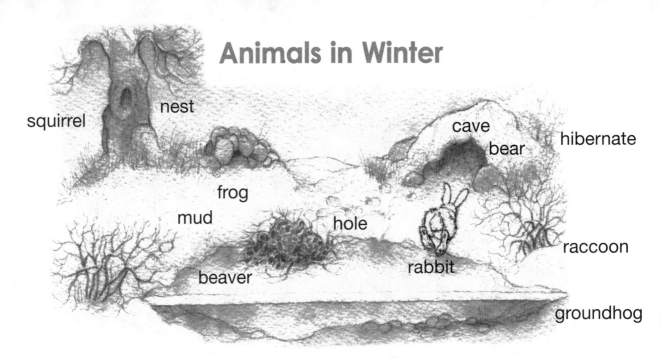

squirrel · nest · frog · mud · beaver · hole · cave · bear · hibernate · raccoon · rabbit · groundhog

1. All of the words in the picture tell about animals in winter. Make a list of words that tell how these animals live through the winter.

2. Match the animal to the place where it sleeps. Write the sentences.

   a) A sleepy bear   spins a cocoon.
   b) A raccoon   sleeps in the mud.
   c) A caterpillar   finds a big cave.
   d) A frog   makes a nest of leaves.
   e) A squirrel   finds a hole in a tree.

3. a) Imagine that you are a sleepy animal looking for a place to spend the winter. What kind of winter home do you need?

   > I am a sleepy _____. I will look for _____ .

   b) Proofread your story with a partner.

58

Grammar Games

Nouns

A **noun** is a kind of word.

Nouns are words that name

people
places
things

My name is **Jerry**.
I'm a **boy**.
I live in a **house**.
I have brown **hair**.
I have big **feet**.

1. Use nouns to finish these sentences.
   Write the sentences in your notebook.

   My name is _____ .
   I am a _____ .
   I live in a _____ .
   I have big _____ .
   I have a black _____ .

2. Write the words in the list below that are nouns.

   cake   and   Pat   the   nose

   ball   bear   go   have   with

Dictionary Games

Summer hot
garden
fan
earth

Autumn fall
hide
exercise
geese

Winter hat
ears
goal
freeze

Spring eggs
helmet
green
flowers

1. a) Find words in the pictures that begin with
e, **f**, **g**, and **h**.

e _____ _____ _____ _____

f _____ _____ _____ _____

g _____ _____ _____ _____

h _____ _____ _____ _____

b) Write sentences using some of the words
you found.

13

Long i
i_e
ri**d**e

time
ride
the
feed
like
sleep
swim
they
five
nine

See the Words

Look carefully at each word in the list.

Say the Words

1. Say the words. Listen for each sound.

   time   ride   like   five   nine

   feed   sleep   the   swim   they

2. Say the words. Listen for the vowel sounds.

 **5** **9**

ride   five   nine

What letters spell the long **i** sound as in **ride**?

✓ Precheck

Check your work. What words do you need to study?

★ Powerbooster ★

The long **i** sound is often spelled **i _ e** as in **ice**, **like**, and **ride**.

59

Write the Words

1. a) Read this story.

   Gina likes to visit her cousin Amy in the country. <u>They</u> <u>swim</u> in the pond and <u>feed</u> the <u>five</u> ducks. Then it is <u>time</u> for dinner. After dinner, Gina and Amy <u>like</u> to <u>ride</u> horses. After such a busy day they are very tired. Sometimes, they go to <u>sleep</u> before <u>nine</u>.

   b) Look for the list words in the story. Write them in your notebook.

2. Write the two list words that have the long **e** sound as in **me**.

   f _ _ d   sl _ _ p

3. Write the words that match the pictures.

   a) t _ m _   b) f _ v _   c) r _ d _   d) n _ n _

4. Write the list words that fit the boxes.

   a)    b)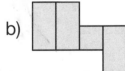

Word Power

1. Write the picture words that rhyme with each list word.

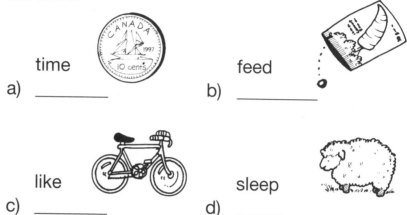

time

a) _____

feed

b) _____

like

c) _____

sleep

d) _____

2. Write the number words from **one** to **ten**. Circle the two words that are list words.

3. Add the letter **h** to the endings **ide**, **ike**, and **ive**. Write the new words in your notebook.

h ⟨ ide = _____
ike = _____
ive = _____

4. Use the new words from exercise 3 to finish these sentences.

a) We went for a _____ in the woods.

b) Bees live in a _____ .

c) They play _____ and seek.

5. Write sentences using these word pairs.

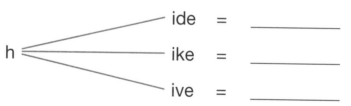

a) they swim   b) like feed

c) time nine

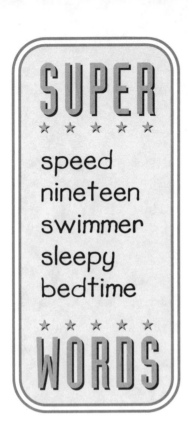

SUPER
★ ★ ★ ★ ★
speed
nineteen
swimmer
sleepy
bedtime
★ ★ ★ ★ ★
WORDS

Challenges with Words

1. a) Write each picture word.

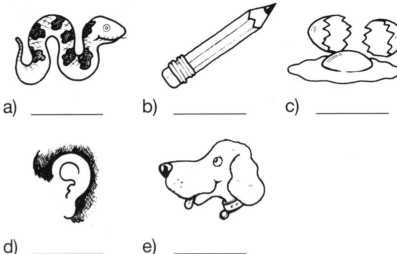

a) _____ b) _____ c) _____

d) _____ e) _____

b) Use the first letter of each word to write a Super Word. __ __ __ __ __

2. Write the Super Words that have the long **e** sound as in **bee** spelled **ee**.

3. Complete each sentence with Super Words.

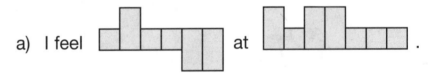

a) I feel [   ] at [   ] .

b) The swi __ __ er was nin __ t __ __ n years old.

4. a) We add **er** to words to tell what someone does.

Example   A **swimmer** is someone who **swims**.

Add **er** to the following words.

farm   sing   dive   dance   run   skip

b) Write a sentence with each new word.

Sometimes I double the last letter before I add **er**. Look at **swimmer**.

5. Write the Super Words that match the clues.

a) [bed image] + time = _____

b) [swimmer image] + er = _____

c) [sleeping image] + y = _____

d) [9 image] + teen = _____

6. Write the Super Word that has three **e**'s and three **n**'s.

7. Write new words by adding **y** to these words.

hair	stick	dirt	frost
dust	snow	mess	cloud

8. Write the words to complete the story.

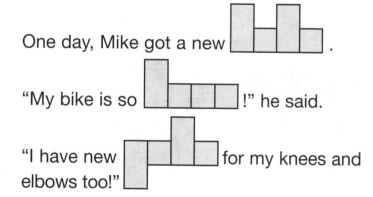

One day, Mike got a new ⬜⬜⬜ .

"My bike is so ⬜⬜⬜⬜ !" he said.

"I have new ⬜⬜⬜ for my knees and elbows too!"

Kids
WORDS

bike
fine
pads

14

Long **u**

o   **ou**   **oo**

d**o**   y**ou**   t**oo**

to
hope
try
too
home
do
by
you
my
your

See the Words

Look at the shape of each word in the list.

Say the Words

1. Listen for each sound as you say each word.

to   do   too   you   my

try   by   home   hope   your

2. Say the words. Listen for the vowel sounds.

do   too   you

What different letters spell the long **u** sound as in **rule**?

✓ Precheck

Check your work. What words do you need to study?

★ Powerbooster ★

Sometimes we use the letters **o**, **ou**, or **oo** to spell long **u** as in **rule**.

Write the Words

1. a) Read the letter Gina sent to Amy.

Dear Amy,

Thank <u>you</u> for asking me to visit <u>your</u> <u>home</u> in the country. I had so much fun. I <u>hope</u> you can visit <u>my</u> house too. There are lots of things to <u>do</u> in the city. <u>Try</u> to come soon.

Your friend,

Gina

P.S. <u>By</u> the way, say "Hi" to your horses for me.

b) Look for the list words in the letter.
Write them in your notebook.

2. Write the four list words that rhyme with **moo**.

3. Write the three list words with the long **i** sound as in **cry**.

4. Find the list words that fit the boxes.
Write the words in your notebook.

a)    b)

65

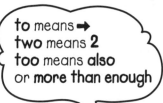

to means ➡
two means **2**
too means **also**
or **more than enough**

Word Power

1. Write these sentences in your notebook.
   Fill in the blanks with **to**, **two**, or **too**.

   a) We are going _____ the store.

   b) May I come _____ ?

   c) No, you are _____ little.

   d) You are only _____ years old.

2. Now write your own sentences with **to**, **two**, and **too**.

3. Match the pairs of rhyming words.
   Write each pair in your notebook.

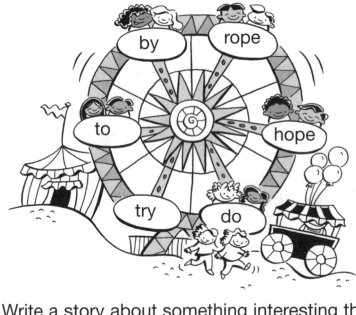

by

rope

to

hope

try

do

4. Write a story about something interesting that happened at your home this week. Use as many list words as you can.

This week _____

_____._____

_____.

Don't forget to proofread your story.

SUPER
★ ★ ★ ★ ★
tooth
loose
cool
mine
yourself
★ ★ ★ ★ ★
WORDS

Challenges with Words

1. Write these sentences in your notebook.
Fill in the blanks with words that rhyme with **mine**.

a) How are you? I am <u>f</u> _ _ _, thank you.

b) I like to paint <u>p</u> _ _ _ cones.

c) The sum of five and four is <u>n</u> _ _ _ .

d) The sun will <u>s</u> <u>h</u> _ _ _ all day.

2. Write rhyming words for each of the words in the centre of the wheels.

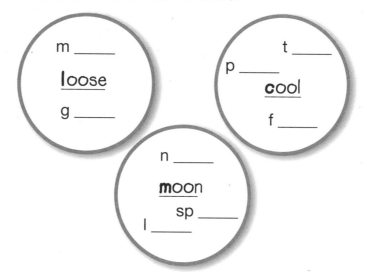

m _____
<u>loose</u>
g _____

t _____
p _____
<u>cool</u>
f _____

n _____
<u>m</u>**oo**<u>n</u>
sp _____
l _____

3. Write a silly sentence with each set of words above.

<u>Example</u>   The fool fell in the cool pool!

4. Read these riddles. Write the missing Super Words in your notebook.

a) I am in a fish's mouth
But not in a bird's
When children lose me
They are glad!
I am a _____ .

b) Gold and silver
Are found in me
I'm very deep.
I am a _____ .

5. a) Some words can be joined with **self** to make compound words. Look at the words in the box.

b) Write the picture sentences in words.
   Fill in the blanks with compound words made with **self**.

Example  am by _myself_ .

I am swinging by myself.

a) [U] are [TV] by _____ .

b) The [face] is [sitting] by _____ .

c) The [boy] is [eating] by _____ .

d) The [chick] is [bird] by _____ .

6. a) Talk about how it feels to have a loose tooth. What might happen when you bite an apple?

b) Write a short story about loosing your first tooth.

68

15

Plurals

s

dog**s**

trees
read
dogs
back
pigs
lots
black
cats
eat
or

See the Words

Look at each word in the list.

Say the Words

1. Say each word. Listen for each sound.

eat   read   cats   back   black

lots   dogs   or   pigs   trees

2. Say the words. Listen for the **last** sounds.

trees   dogs   cats

What letter tells you that a word means
more than one?

✓ Precheck

**Check your work.
Write the words
you misspelled.**

★ Powerbooster ★

We add **s** to some words to show that there are
more than one as in **dogs** and **cats**. It sounds
like **s** or **z**. We call these words **plurals**.

Write the Words

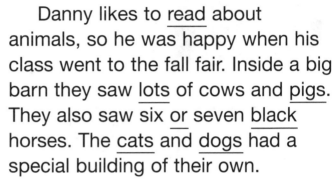

1. a) Read this story.

Danny likes to <u>read</u> about animals, so he was happy when his class went to the fall fair. Inside a big barn they saw <u>lots</u> of cows and <u>pigs</u>. They also saw six or seven <u>black</u> horses. The <u>cats</u> and <u>dogs</u> had a special building of their own.

On the way <u>back</u> to school their bus stopped at a park so they could <u>eat</u> lunch under the <u>trees</u>. Danny said it was a really good <u>trip</u>!

b) Look for the list words in the story.
Write the words in your notebook.

2. Write the five list words that mean **more than one**.

3. Write the three list words with the long **e** sound as in **me**. Circle the word with long **e** spelled **ee**. Underline the words with long **e** spelled **ea**.

4. Write the list words that rhyme with the words under the pictures.

track   door   bead   seat

Word Power

1. Make new words by adding the letters on the wheels to the beginning of **eat** and **eed**. Write them in your notebook.

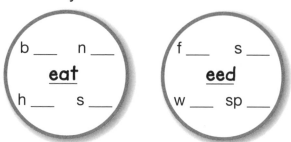

b ___   n ___
eat
h ___   s ___

f ___   s ___
eed
w ___   sp ___

2. Complete each math problem. Write the answers in your notebook.

a)   +   =   _four dogs_

b)   +   =   _____

c)   +   =   _____

d)   +   =   _____

3. Use each pair of words in a sentence.

a) black back   b) read or   c) eat lots

SUPER
★ ★ ★ ★ ★
monsters
dreams
peanuts
backyard
picnic
★ ★ ★ ★ ★
WORDS

Challenges with Words

1. Write the Super Words that match these clues.

   a) This word has two **c**'s and two **i**'s.

   b) These words are compound words.

   c) These words have the long **e** sound as in **me**.

2. Write these words in alphabetical order.

   balloons   hats   pigs   kites   cars

   trees   dogs   ships   apples   jets

3. Write these sentences in your notebook.
   Fill in the blanks with Super Words.

   a) Last night I had bad ◯ _ _ _ _ _ .

   b) Elephants love _ _ _ _ ◯ _ _ .

   c) The children had a _ _ ◯ _ _ _ .

   d) There's a swing in our _ _ _ ◯ _ _ _ _ .

   e) Here come big, blue _ _ _ ◯ _ _ _ _ !

4. The circled letters in the words in exercise 3
   make a hidden word. Use it to finish this
   sentence.

   We went to the pond to feed the _ _ _ _ _ .

72

It **seems** the **seams** have come undone!

5. Make words using the word wheel.
Write the words in your notebook.

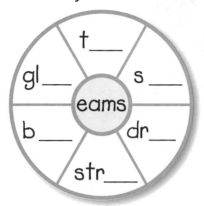

t___
gl___
s ___
eams
b ___
dr___
str___

6. What would happen if a monster turned up in your backyard?

Write a story about a surprise monster. What does it look like? What colour is it?

7. Unscramble the words in these sentences. Write them in your notebook.

a) I like to watch tncorsoa.

b) She likes to mooz around on her bike.

c) We got free oosbnlal at the new store.

Kids
WORDS

zoom
balloons
cartoon

73

16

Long **a**
ay
pl**ay**

play
she
day
away
girl
way
boy
may
dad
mom

See the Words

Look carefully at each list word.

Say the Words

1. Say each word. Listen for each sound.

may   way   away   day   play

boy   girl   she   mom   dad

2. Say the words. Listen for the vowel sounds.

play   stay   jay

What letters spell the long **a** sound as in **day**?

✓ Precheck

Check your work. What words do you need to study?

★ Powerbooster ★

When the long **a** comes at the end of a word, it is often spelled with the letters **ay**.

Write the Words

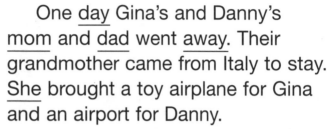

1. a) Read this story.

One <u>day</u> Gina's and Danny's <u>mom</u> and <u>dad</u> went <u>away</u>. Their grandmother came from Italy to stay. <u>She</u> brought a toy airplane for Gina and an airport for Danny.

"<u>May</u> I <u>play</u> with your airplane?" asked Danny.

"Can I play with your airport?" asked Gina.

Grandmother laughed. "That's a good <u>way</u> to get along. I like to see a <u>girl</u> and <u>boy</u> play together"

b) Look for the list words in the story. Write them in your notebook.

2. Write the two pairs of list words that are opposites.

3. Write the list words that rhyme with the pictures.

4. Write the list words that have long **a** spelled **ay**.

Word Power

1. Write this picture verse in words.
   Fill in the missing letters.

A little 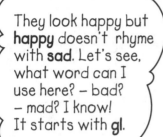 ran a _ _ y.

S _ _ went 2 a park 2 p _ _ y.

Her [girl] and [man] were very [sad] .

Then s _ _ came [house] .

And they were [happy] [happy] .

They look happy but **happy** doesn't rhyme with **sad**. Let's see, what word can I use here? – bad? – mad? I know! It starts with **gl**.

2. Write new words by adding the letters on each point of the stars to **ay** and **ad**.

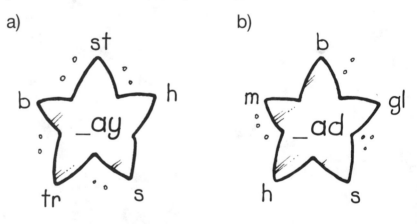

a)

st
b   h
_ay
tr   s

b)

b
m   gl
_ad
h   s

3. Write sentences or a poem with words that end in **ay**. Use list words, words from this page, or other **ay** words you can think of.

SUPER

★ ★ ★ ★ ★

playground
clay
parents
crayon
daytime

★ ★ ★ ★ ★

WORDS

Colours. I love colours.

Challenges with Words

1. Write the Super Words that have the long **a** sound spelled **ay** as in **day**.

2. Write the Super Words that are compounds.

3. Write the colour words that match the clues below.

Colour	Clues
a) _____	rhymes with **pack** the colour of night
b) _____	rhymes with **glue** the colour of the sky
c) _____	has the long **i** sound the colour of snow
d) _____	has the long **e** sound the colour of grass

4. Write these picture sentences in words.

a) We use ⬛ and ☁ to make 🎁 for our 👫 .

b) 🅄🧵 go 2 the 🛝 .

5. Make as many small words as you can with the letters of the word **playground**.

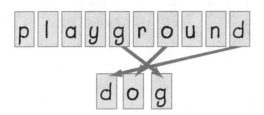

6. Write the names of the parents of these animal babies. If you need help, look in a book about animals.

cow   calf

kitten	cat	calf	_____
puppy	_____	kid	_____
foal	_____	cub	_____
chick	_____	fawn	_____
lamb	_____	piglet	_____

7. What is your favourite colour? Make a book of things in your favourite colour.

Write about something different on each page.

78

17

Two Syllable Words
sis ter

father
pets
mother
girls
other
say
brother
hay
sister
boys

See the Words

Look at the shape of each list word.

Say the Words

1. Say the words. Listen carefully for each sound.

    mother   brother   other   father   sister

    say   hay   boys   girls   pets

2. Say the words. Listen for the number of word parts.

mother   sister   brother

How many vowel sounds do these words have?

✓ Precheck

Check your work. Underline the parts of the words you need to study.

★ Powerbooster ★

Many words have **two parts** that you can hear as in **mother** and **father**. Each part is called a **syllable**.

79

Write the Words

1. a) Read this story.

There are five people in my family — my <u>mother</u>, my <u>father</u>, my <u>brother</u>, Jeff, my <u>sister</u>, Janet, and me! My father lives in another town. We live in the country and have many <u>pets</u>. Other <u>boys</u> and <u>girls</u> come here to ride our horses and to play in the <u>hay</u>. They <u>say</u> they have lots of fun.

b) Look for all the list words in the story. Write them in your notebook.

2. a) Write the three list words that mean **more than one**.

b) Write the letter you see at the end of these words.

3. Write two list words that rhyme with **day**.

4. Write the five list words that have two syllables.

<u>f</u> _ <u>t</u> _ _ _   <u>m</u> _ _ <u>h</u> _ _

<u>o</u> _ _ _ <u>r</u>   <u>b</u> <u>r</u> _ _ <u>h</u> _ _

<u>s</u> _ <u>s</u> _ _ _

Word Power

1. Say the words. Write the words that have two syllables.

farmer   car   pumpkin   pencil   bee   dragon

2. Write these picture sentences in words.

a) The  and  are reading  .

b) The 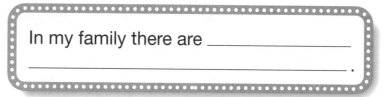 chase the 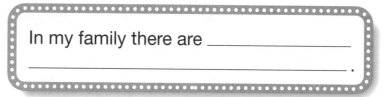 up the 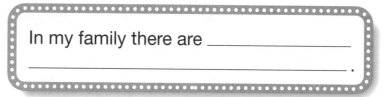 .

3. Write the words you can make with the word wheel.

4. Choose three words from exercise 3. Write a sentence with each word.

Read your sentences to a partner.

5. a) Write a sentence about the people in your family.

In my family there are _____
_____ .

b) Write a short story about something funny that happened in your family. Share it with a partner.

81

SUPER
★ ★ ★ ★ ★
grandmother
stepfather
fingers
numbers
giants
★ ★ ★ ★ ★
WORDS

Challenges with Words

1. Write the Super Words that have two syllables.

2. Write the Super Words that have three syllables.

3. Unscramble the words below. Use the words to fill in the blanks in the sentences. Write them in your notebook.

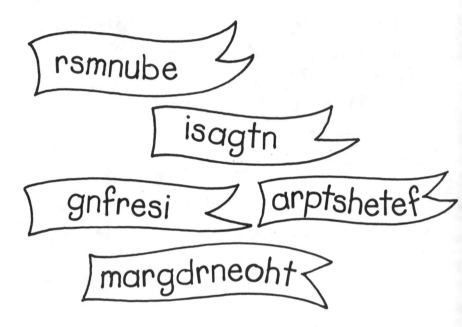

rsmnube

isagtn

gnfresi

arptshetef

margdrneoht

If two words have the same **first** letter, look at the **second** letter to put them in alphabetical order.

a) That man is my _____ .
b) The _____ lived in a very large castle.
c) I have ten toes and ten _____ .
d) It is fun to make codes with _____ .
e) Little Red Riding Hood went to see her _____.

4. Now write your own sentences with the Super Words. You can use more than one word in a sentence.

5. Write the Super Words in alphabetical order.

6. Join the words in box A with the words in box B to make compound words. Write as many words as you can.

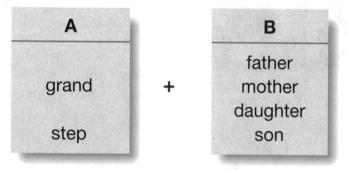

A		B
		father
grand	**+**	mother
		daughter
step		son

7. a) Find a story that begins **Once upon a time**. Read it to a partner.

b) Write a story that starts with **Once upon a time.** You may want to use list words, Super Words, or Kids Words.

> Once upon a time there was
> _____
> _____ .
>
> She/He/It lived _____
> _____ .
>
> One day _____
> _____ .

8. All the Kids Words are names of birds. Fill in the missing letters in the words below.

a) The <u>c</u> _ _ <u>w</u> says "caw-caw."

b) We saw a beautiful <u>b</u> _ _ _ <u>j</u> _ <u>y</u> in our yard.

c) The <u>b</u> <u>l</u> _ _ <u>k</u> <u>b</u> _ _ <u>d</u> sings in the spring.

18

Looking Back

Here is a list of words from Units 12–17 that may be hard for you.

away	to	back	two
they	girls	too	brother
read	the	like	home

look

say

cover

write

check

1. Follow the Study Steps for each word in the list.

2. Write this story in your notebook.
   Fill in the blanks with **to**, **too**, or **two**.

   Toula heard something at the door. She went
   _____ the door. It was _____ dark
   _____ see. She went _____ the window
   _____ look out. _____ of her friends were
   standing on the steps. They wanted _____
   come in. It was _____ cold to be outside.

3. Write the picture words that have the long **i**
   sound as in **ice**.

n _ _ _   sm _ _ _   t _ _ _

sl _ _ _   f _ _ _   p_ _ _

4. What letters can you use to spell the long **i**?

5. Write the words from the list below that have the long **u** sound as in **rule**.

you   but   too   until   upon   two

to   door   blue   your   just   do

6. All of the picture words have the long **a** sound. Write the words.

c _ _ _   pl _ _   h _ _

c _ _ _   p _ _   sn _ _ _ _

A word that means **more than one** is a **plural**.

7. What two ways can you spell the long **a** sound?

8. Complete these sentences with words that mean **more than one**.

a) The [picture] and [picture] are happy.

b) We have [picture] and [picture] for p _ t _ .

c) Here are some [picture] to read.

9. Write the words in the box that have two vowel sounds you can hear.

target	green	baby	mother
jump	other	farm	girl
father	away	black	funny

10. Write five words from your math book that have two syllables.

11. Write the words in your notebook that fit the puzzle. Use the clues to help you.

a) the opposite of work
b) the chicken will _____ an egg
c) the opposite of night
d) something you colour with
e) the opposite of go
f) what horses eat

12. Make your own review list. Use list words, Super Words, Kids Words, or words from your Personal Word List. Get a partner to dictate your words to you.

Don't forget to use the five Study Steps!

It's Riddle Time

Humpty Dumpty sat on a wall,
Humpty Dumpty had a great fall,
All the king's horses and all the
 king's men
Couldn't put Humpty together again.

1. This is an old riddle. What is Humpty Dumpty?
_ <u>n</u> _ _ <u>g</u>

2. Can you guess this riddle?
Riddle me! riddle me!
What is that:
Over your head and
under your hat?
<u>h</u> _ _ <u>r</u>

Here's my favourite riddle. What's grey, has four legs and a trunk?
Answer: a mouse going on a holiday.

3. Now it's your turn to write riddles. Read the example. Then write riddles for the answers below or make up your own.

a) <u>What's white, cold, and round?</u> (a snowball)

b) _____ (a school bus)

c) _____ (a kangaroo)

d) _____ (a doughnut)

e) _____ (a bar of soap)

f) _____ (a rocket)

g) _____ (an elephant)

4. Make a riddle book. Write and illustrate some of your favourite riddles.

Grammar Games

Adjectives

An **adjective** tells about a noun.

Size

| tall | short | big | small | long |

Colour

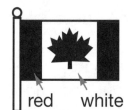 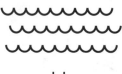

red   white   green   blue

Shape

round   square   curly

1. Use adjectives to finish these sentences.

    a) I have _____ eyes.
    b) I have _____ hair.
    c) I have _____ shoes.
    d) My pencil is _____ .

2. Write these sentences in the correct order.

    a) big   love   I   apples.   red
    b) ball.   has   She   a   small
    c) candies.   We   pink   like
    d) He   green   has   eyes.

Dictionary Games

1. Find words in the pictures that begin with **i**, **j**, **k**, and **l**.

i _____ _____ _____

j _____ _____ _____ _____

k _____ _____ _____ _____

l _____ _____ _____ _____

2. Look on page 171 of this book. Write two more words that begin with each of these letters.

i _____ _____   **k** _____ _____

j _____ _____   **l** _____ _____

87b

19

Consonant Sound
th
this

this
come
there
fish
that
some
wish
look
their
took

See the Words

Look at each word in the list.

Say the Words

1. Say each word. Listen for each sound.

   this   that   there   their   took

   look   wish   fish   some   come

2. Say the words. Listen for the sound at the beginning of each word.

   this   that   there   their

   What letters make the beginning sound?

✓ Precheck

Check your work. Write the words you misspelled.

★ Powerbooster ★

When we say the sound **th** as in **the**, we spell it with the letters **th**.

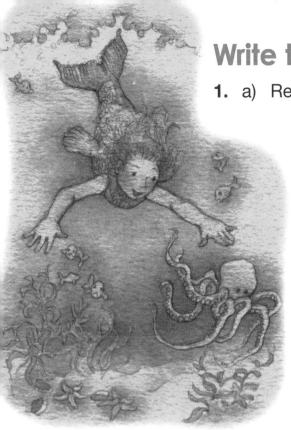

Write the Words

1. a) Read this verse.

I <u>wish</u> I were a little <u>fish</u> swimming in the sea.
I wish <u>that</u> all my friends could <u>come</u> and share <u>this</u> swim with me.
I wish <u>some</u> sharks would smile at us as they went swimming past.
<u>Their</u> teeth <u>look</u> awfully sharp and white, (I'm glad they're swimming fast).
I wish <u>there</u> were an octopus who <u>took</u> us home with him.
And showed us how he learned to use eight wiggly arms to swim!

b) Look for all the list words in the poem. Write them in your notebook.

2. Write the two list words that sound exactly the same.

3. Write the three pairs of list words that rhyme.

4. Write the two list words that have the short **u** sound as in **cup**.

5. Write the list words that fit the boxes. Circle the letters that make the sound **th**.

Both words rhyme with **hum**.

a) 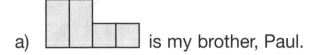 is my brother, Paul.

b) May I have some of 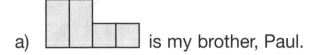 cake, please?

Word Power

1. Read these sentences. See how **there** and **their** are used.

There are lots of trees over **there**.

Their bikes are yellow and black.

Complete these sentences with **there** or **their**.

a) Are you going _____ today?

b) The boys and girls play with _____ pets.

c) _____ are three toys in the box.

2. Write the picture words that rhyme with each list word.

a) wish

b) look

c) that

3. a) Complete these sentences with your own wishes.

I wish I were a _____.

I wish I could have _____.

I wish I could go _____.

b) Draw a picture to go with one of your sentences.

Challenges with Words

1. The fisher wants to catch one fish at a time.
Write the words on the fish in alphabetical order.

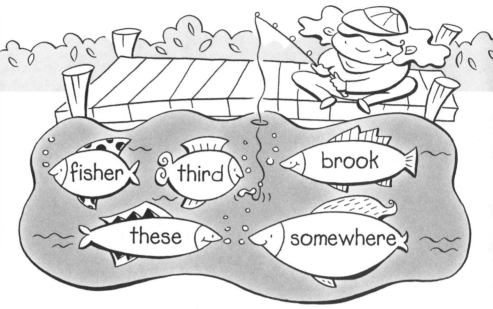

Hint! If two words
have the same **second**
letter, look at the **third**
letter to put them in
alphabetical order!

2. Use the clues to find words that rhyme with
brook. Write the words.

a) to make dinner   _____
b) use this to catch fish   _____
c) has stories in it   _____
d) to use your eyes   _____

3. Find the Super Words that fit the boxes.
Write each sentence.

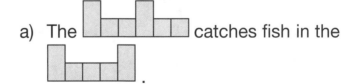

a) The ⬚⬚⬚⬚⬚⬚ catches fish in the
⬚⬚⬚⬚⬚ .

b) I will put ⬚⬚⬚⬚ toys ⬚⬚⬚⬚⬚⬚⬚⬚⬚ .

c) He was ⬚⬚⬚⬚⬚ in the race.

91

4. a) Write the Super Words that rhyme with these picture words.

b) Write a sentence with each word.

5. Look at the picture. Answer the questions below with a sentence. Write the sentences.

a) Who is second in line? <u>Claire is second.</u>
b) Who is first in line? _____
c) Who is fifth in line? _____
d) Who is third in line? _____
e) Who is fourth in line? _____

6. This fisher thinks he has a big fish on his hook. Write about what you think is going to happen next.

7. Unscramble the fishing words below.

a) I have a new fishing **ord**.
b) My **eiln** is very strong.
c) Put the **mrsow** on the hook.

20

Compound Words
something

house
yesterday
outside
mouse
his
today
her
something
birthday
sometimes

See the Words

Look carefully at each list word.

Say the Words

1. Say the words. Listen for each sound.

   mouse house outside his her

   today birthday yesterday sometimes

   something

2. Say the words. Listen for two shorter words in each word.

   outside birthday something sometimes

   Sometimes it is easier to spell a **compound word** like **something** if you say each part by itself before you write it as one word.

✓ Precheck

Check your work. Underline the parts of words you need to study.

★ Powerbooster ★

Compound words are made up of two shorter words like **something** and **birthday**.

Write the Words

1. a) Read this verse.

In our <u>house</u>
There lives a <u>mouse</u>.
I saw <u>her</u> <u>yesterday</u>.
She came <u>outside</u> to take a peek
While others were away.
<u>Sometimes</u> she looks for water
Or <u>something</u> good to eat.
I'll leave some bread and cheese <u>today</u>
So she will have a treat.

b) Look for the list words in the verse.
Write them in your notebook.

c) Write the two list words that are not in
the verse.

2. Write the compound words from the word list.
Draw a box around the two smaller words in
each compound word.

Example

3. Write the picture words. Circle the letters that
are the same.

4. Complete the sentences with list words.

David and Diane are twins. _____ birthday
and _____ birthday are on the same day.

Word Power

1. Write compound words for the pictures below.

a)  _____

b)  _____

c)  _____

d)  _____

2. Draw two pictures for each compound word.

doghouse   cupcake   toothbrush

3. Complete the sentences with list words.

a) The m_ _s_ ran _ _ _ side
   the h_ _ _ _ .

b) T_d_ _ is my b_ _ _ _ d_ _ .

c) Y_ _t_ _d_ _ I did s_m_t_ing well.

4. Write a story about the best birthday you ever
   had. You might need words like these.

happy   cake   special   older

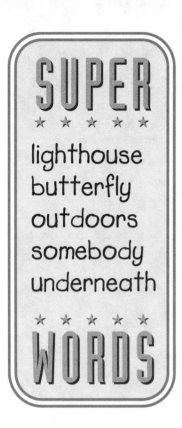

SUPER
★ ★ ★ ★ ★

lighthouse
butterfly
outdoors
somebody
underneath

★ ★ ★ ★ ★

WORDS

Challenges with Words

1. Make compound words with **some**.
   Write them in your notebook.

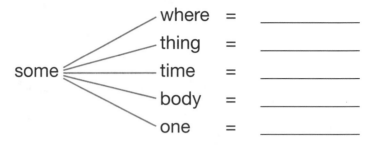

some
- where = _____
- thing = _____
- time = _____
- body = _____
- one = _____

2. Write a sentence with two of the words you have made in exercise 1.

3. Look at the picture carefully.

Complete the sentences that tell where the Big Bad Wolf and the Three Little Pigs are. Use these words.

inside   outdoors   underneath   upstairs

a) The wolf is _____ .
b) The three pigs are _____ the house.
c) The wolf is _____ the tree.
d) One little pig is _____ .

4. Write the compound words with **house.**

a) _____ + _____ = _____

b) _____ + _____ = _____

c) _____ + _____ = _____

d) _____ + _____ = _____

5. Solve the riddles. The answers are compound words. Write the answers.

a) I start my life as a caterpillar.
I have beautiful wings.
What am I? _____

b) I am full of sand.
Children play in me.
What am I? _____

c) I am a man who melts on
a warm sunny day.
What am I? _____

d) I have large wings.
People fly in me.
What am I? _____

6. Choose three compound words. Write your own riddles about them. Read your riddles to a partner.

21

Base Words and Endings

–s   **–ing**

make**s**   play**ing**

them
walking
then
playing
makes
fishing
comes
going
give
live

See the Words

Look carefully at the words in the list.

Say the Words

1. Say each list word. Listen for each sound.

   them   then   give   live   going

   fishing   walking   playing   makes   comes

2. Say the words. Listen for the **-ing** endings.
   going   fishing   playing   walking

3. Say the words. Listen for the **-s** endings.
   makes   comes

☑ Precheck

Check your work. What words do you need to study?

★ Powerbooster ★

We call the part of a word we add an ending to a **base word.**   walk + -ing = walking

base word   ending

Write the Words

1. a) Read the story.

Amy and her dad are <u>going</u> <u>fishing</u>. They pack a lunch and <u>then</u> off they go. They are <u>walking</u> to their fishing spot. Amy's dad is lucky to <u>live</u> near a river.

They fish all day but they only catch two little fish. This is not <u>playing</u>, this is hard work!

Evening <u>comes</u> and Amy and her dad are glad to <u>give</u> up and go home for dinner. Fishing <u>makes</u> <u>them</u> hungry!

b) Look for all the list words in the story. Write them in your notebook.

2. Write the two list words that fit this box.

Underline the word that rhymes with **men**.

3. Write the four list words that end in **-ing**. Put a box around the base words.

Example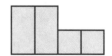

4. Write the two list words that end in **-s**. Underline the base words.

5. Write the word **walk**. Say it. Underline the letter you do not hear.

Word Power

1. Add the endings **-ing** and **-s** to these base words. Write the words.

    a) kick   <u>kicking</u>   <u>kicks</u>

    b) talk   _____   _____

    c) eat   _____   _____

    d) work   _____   _____

    e) jump   _____   _____

2. Write these picture sentences in words.

    a) The  are j__m p__ __g up and down.

    b) My mother w__ __ks to work.

    c)  went ... yesterday.

3. Find the list words that fit these boxes. Write the words in your notebook.

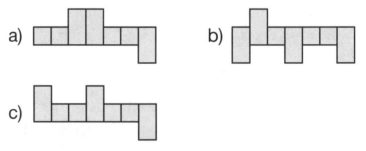

    a)

    b)

    c)

Underline the base words.

4. a) Use each pair of words in a sentence.

    going   fishing   playing   walking

    b) Read your sentences to a partner.

SUPER WORDS

speaking
talking
whispering
asks
goldfish

Challenges with Words

1. Complete these sentences with Super Words.

   a) My _____ is swimming in its bowl.

   b) You are s p _ _ k _ _ _ too softly.

   c) The children are _____ secrets.

   d) Quiet! You are t _ _ k _ _ _ too much.

   e) That boy _____ a lot of questions.

2. Unscramble the words in the goldfish bowl.

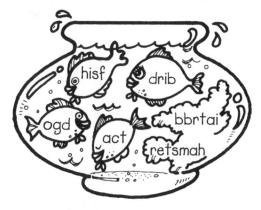

hisf   drib   ogd   act   bbrtai   retsmah

Hint! They are all names of pets.

3. Choose one of the pets from exercise 2.
   Tell how to take care of this pet.
   Make a list of four things to do.

How to care for a _____
1. _____
2. _____
3. _____
4. _____

101

4. Add **-ing** and **-s** endings to these base words to make words that tell how we can use our voices.

	-ing	**-s**
a)	shout _____	shout _____
b)	cheer _____	cheer _____
c)	scream _____	scream _____
d)	whisper _____	whisper _____

Hint! There can be more than one right answer.

5. Use the words above and Super Words to complete these sentences.

a) My friend _____ so no one can hear her.

b) When Jacob scored a goal, everyone was _____ and _____ .

c) Dad _____ when he hits his thumb.

6. These cartoons have animals speaking. Write what you think each animal might be saying.

7. Write words that fit these boxes. The picture clues will help.

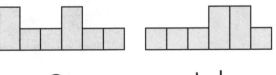

Kids WORDS

tastes
smells
feels

102

22

Base Words and Endings
-ing
rid**ing**

was
with
were
riding
are
coming
plays
likes
swimming
for

See the Words

1. Look at each word in the list.

2. Look at these words.

   ride riding   come coming

   What happened to the base words **ride** and **come** when **-ing** was added?

3. Look at these words.

   swim swimming   hit hitting

   What happened to the base words **swim** and **hit** when **-ing** was added?

Say the Words

Say each word. Listen for each sound.

riding   coming   swimming   plays   likes

was   with   were   are   for

✓ Precheck

Check your work. Write the words you misspelled.

★ Powerbooster ★

When adding **-ing** to some words
• the final **e** is dropped, as in **ride—riding**.
• the final letter is doubled, as in **swim—swimming**.

Write the Words

1. a) Read this story.

My best friend Mark <u>plays</u> <u>with</u> me every day. We have fun <u>riding</u> our bikes and going <u>swimming</u>. Mark likes <u>coming</u> to my house <u>for</u> lunch. Last week he <u>was</u> sick and we <u>were</u> both lonely. Now Mark is <u>better</u> and we <u>are</u> having fun again.

b) Look for all the list words in the story. Write them in your notebook.

2. a) Write the list word for each of the pictures.

Hint: It rhymes with **car**!

b) Now write the three base words.

3. Write the three list words that begin with **w**.

4. Write the list word that sounds like a letter of the alphabet.

Word Power

1. Add **-ing** to these base words. Write the words.

   make   making   hope   hoping

   save   hide   dive   bike   take

2. Add **-ing** to these base words. Write the words.

   swim   swimming   get   sit   pet

   hit   hitting   hop   tap   rap

3. Write these sentences in your notebook.

   a)   and   are fun.

   b) We like   and   .

4. Write the list words that begin with two consonant letters.

5. a) Use each pair of words in a sentence.

   likes   for   are   coming   plays   with

   b) Make a picture to go with one of your sentences.

SUPER

★ ★ ★ ★ ★

smiling
hugging
crown
without
forget

★ ★ ★ ★ ★

WORDS

Watch for words
that double the
final letter or
drop an **e**
before **-ing**!

Challenges with Words

1. Complete the sentences with Super Words.

    Write the sentences in your notebook.

    a) The king won't
        _ _ _ _ _ _ to wear his c _ _ _ _ n.

    b) The woman is s _ _ l _ _ _ and
        h _ g _ _ _ _ her children.

    c) Don't go out w _ _ h _ _ t your cap!

2. Add **-ing** to these base words. Write the words.

    share hop pon slip live skate dance give hug save **-ing**

3. Write new words by changing the consonant blend at the beginning of **crown**. Use these clues to help you.

    a) The opposite of a smile is a _____ .

    b) A person who makes you laugh at a circus is a _____ .

    c) The colour of chocolate is often _____ .

4. Build words on the letters of the word **smiling**. Use the names of people or things that make you smile. The first one is done for you.

```
s m i l i n g
t
a
r
s
```

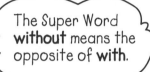

5. Write the opposites of the words below.

a) happy _____   e) taking _____

b) going _____   f) playing _____

c) sister _____   g) father _____

d) remember _____   h) boy _____

6. Unscramble the Super Words. Write a sentence with each one.

ughngig   gimlins

totuiwh   ergoft   wronc

7. a) Write a true story about a day you will never forget. Think of an exciting sentence to begin your story.

   b) Share ideas with a partner to make your story even better.

Contractions
don't

when
where
morning
I'm
don't
it's
didn't
that's
said
found

See the Words

1. Look at each word in the list.

2. Look carefully at these words.

I'm   don't   it's   didn't   that's

These words are called **contractions**.

3. Look at the words and the **contractions**. What letter has been left out in each one?

do not — don't   did not — didn't
 it is — it's   I am — I'm

What mark do we use to show where a letter has been left out?

Say the Words

Say each word. Listen for each sound.

when   where   it's   that's   didn't

don't   I'm   found   morning   said

☑ Precheck

Check your work. Underline the parts of the words you need to study.

★ Powerbooster ★

When we write **contractions** such as **I'm** and **it's**, we use a special mark called an apostrophe **'**.

Write the Words

1. a) Read this conversation between Danny and Mark.

> Danny: Where are you going Mark?
> Mark: I'm going to the store. My parents need some bread.
> Danny: When will you be back?
> Mark: I don't know. It's a long walk and I didn't bring my bike.
> Danny: I'll come too. I found a quarter this morning, and my Dad said I could spend it.
> Mark: That's great. Let's go!

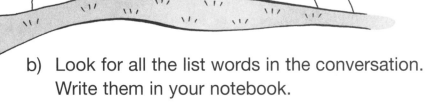

b) Look for all the list words in the conversation. Write them in your notebook.

2. Write the two list words that you can use to ask questions.

3. Write the five list words that are contractions.

4. Write the list word that means the opposite of **lost**.

5. Write the list word that rhymes with **red**. Circle the letters that make the short **e** sound.

Word Power

1. Write contractions for the underlined words below.
   a) I am glad you did not go there.
   b) We do not think it is a good plan.
   c) That is my dog.
   d) Today was not sunny.

2. Make new words using **ound** as in **found**.

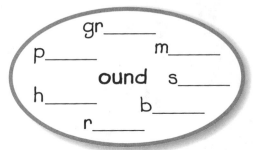

   gr_____
   p_____   m_____
   ound   s_____
   h_____   b_____
   r_____

3. Use **when** and **where** in these sentences. Write the sentences in your notebook.
   a) Do you know _____ Mom is coming home?
   b) I know _____ my book is.
   c) Jill doesn't know _____ to put her coat.
   d) I know _____ Sheldon is coming back to school.

4. a) Write a conversation between you and a friend. Use Danny's conversation as an example.
   b) Read your conversation out loud with a partner.

   _____   Hi! Where _____
   (Your name)
   _____?

   _____   I'm _____
   (Friend's name)
   _____.

SUPER
★ ★ ★ ★ ★

who's
where's
says
answer
groundhog

★ ★ ★ ★ ★

WORDS

Challenges with Words

1. Many question words make contractions with the word **is**. Write the contractions for these words.

   a) who is
   b) what is
   c) where is
   d) how is

2. Complete these sentences with the contractions in exercise 1.

   a) _____ your new puppy's name?
   b) _____ Sandy going this morning?
   c) _____ knocking at the front door?
   d) _____ your sister feeling?

3. Write the words **says** and **said**. Circle the letters that make the short **e** sound.

4. Complete the sentences with **says** or **said**.

   a) Yesterday Jared_____ he found a dollar.
   b) My Dad always _____ "Don't give up."
   c) The clock _____ three-thirty now.
   d) This morning my friend _____ she would wait for me.

It's fun to say tongue twisters fast.

5. Write the Super Word that has a silent letter. Circle the letter.

6. a) Say this silly tongue twister.

   How much ground could a groundhog grind
   If a groundhog could grind ground?
   A groundhog could grind,
   As much ground as a groundhog could grind,
   If a groundhog could grind ground!

7. Match the pictures and words below to make animal names that are compound words.

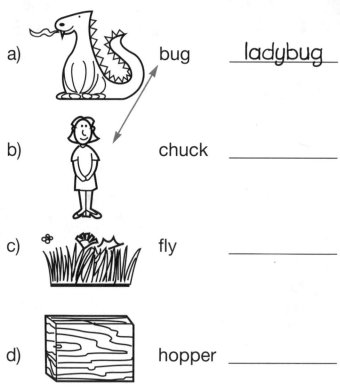

a) bug   <u>ladybug</u>

b) chuck _____

c) fly _____

d) hopper _____

Kids WORDS

please
thank you
you're
welcome

8. You need these words to sound polite. Unscramble the words to complete the sentences.

a) knhta oyu for the ice cream, Joe.

b) oyu'er elwemoc, Leslie.

c) eplase have some more.

24

STUDY STEPS

look

say

cover

write

check

Looking Back

Here are some words from Units 19–23 that may be hard for you.

don't	didn't	something	were
when	it's	sometimes	their
where	them	there	then
going	swimming	said	are

1. Follow the Study Steps for each review word.

2. Write two words for each contraction.

   Example   we're   **we are**

don't	you're	it's
let's	who's	didn't
there's	wasn't	hasn't

3. Write the contractions for these words.

Meaning	Contraction
a) I am	_____
b) it is	_____
c) that is	_____
d) did not	_____
e) do not	_____

this	them
there	then
that	their
there's	

4. The words in the box all begin with the sound **th** as in **then**. Complete the sentences below with the correct words and write them in your notebook.

a) T _ _ _ _ _ s my bike over t _ _ _ _ e.

b) We gave t _ _ _ _ r books to t _ _ _ m.

c) Is t _ _ _ t your toy car?

d) T _ _ s girl took my hat, t _ _ _ n ran away.

5. Copy this chart in your notebook. Fill in the blanks by spelling the base word, the **-s** ending word, or the **-ing** ending word.

Base Word	-s Word	-ing Word
come	comes	_____
make	_____	
_____	gives	giving
live	_____	_____
play	_____	_____
ride	rides	_____

6. Join the picture words.
Write the compound words in your notebook.

a)  = _____

b)  = _____

c)  = _____

7. Join the base words to make compound words.
Write the words in your notebook.
The first one is done for you.

a) every   side   _everything_

b) birth   times   _____

c) some   plane   _____

d) in   thing   _____

e) air   day   _____

8. Write these sentences in words. Use all the clues.

a) I like [fish] + ing and [swim] + ing.

b) Can [U] come [2] my [house] today?

c) [eye] [can] [C] their [dog]

out + side.

Don't forget! Follow the Study Steps.

9. Make your own review list. Add words from the Unit Tests and your Personal Word List. Get a partner to dictate your words to you.

Storms

wind

blizzard   cold

thunder   dark clouds

ice

lightning

hurricane   blowing

spray

waves

snow   hail   swaying   wet

rain

1. Many parts of Canada have storms. What are the storms like where you live? Make a class list of storm words.

2. We use many interesting words to tell about storms.

   a) Write four words for a rainstorm.

   b) Write four words for a windstorm.

   c) Write four words for a snowstorm.

3. Write about the worst storm you have ever seen. Read your report to a partner or record it on tape. Talk about ways you could make your report even better.

raindrops
big gusts
snowflakes

Grammar Games

Verbs

Verbs tell us about things we do.

run   swing   ride   eat

Verbs tell us about how we are and how we feel.

She **is** a skater.   He **loves** ice cream.

1. Add verbs from the box to complete these sentences. Write the sentences in your notebook.

ride
like
go
come

a) The girls _____ their bikes.

b) I _____ hot dogs.

c) Please, _____ with me.

d) What time do you _____ to school?

2. Write your own sentences with these verbs.

walk   play   looks   love

Dictionary Games

1. Write the words in the nature setting that begin with **m**, **n**, **o**, and **p**.

    m _____ _____ _____

    n _____ _____ _____

    o _____ _____ _____

    p _____ _____ _____

2. Look on page 171 of this book. Write your two favourite words that begin with each of these letters.

    m _____ _____   o _____ _____

    n _____ _____   p_____ _____

25

Base Words and Endings
-ed
ask**ed** liv**ed**

can't
friend
asked
let's
thing
played
airplane
looked
put
lived
truck

See the Words

1. Look at the shape of each word in the list.

2. Look at these words.

   lived   played   asked   looked

   What has been added to the base words
   live, **play**, **ask**, **look**?
   Lived has a base word ending in **e**. What
   happened to the **e** in **live** when **-ed** was added?

Say the Words

Say each word. Listen for each sound.

lived   played   asked   looked   can't

let's   airplane   truck   put   thing   friend

✓ Precheck

**Check your work.
What words do
you need to study?**

★ Powerbooster ★

When you add **-ed** to a word ending in **e**, one **e**
is dropped.

Write the Words

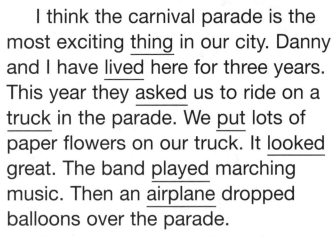

1. a) Read this story.

> I think the carnival parade is the most exciting <u>thing</u> in our city. Danny and I have <u>lived</u> here for three years. This year they <u>asked</u> us to ride on a <u>truck</u> in the parade. We <u>put</u> lots of paper flowers on our truck. It <u>looked</u> great. The band <u>played</u> marching music. Then an <u>airplane</u> dropped balloons over the parade.
>
> "<u>Let's</u> get a balloon," our <u>friend</u> shouted.
>
> I <u>can't</u> wait for next year's parade.

b) Look for the list words in the story.
Write them in your notebook.

2. Write the contractions that mean the same as the underlined words.

a) <u>Let us</u> go out to play.

b) I <u>can not</u> go until I have made my bed.

3. Write the list words ending in **-ed**.

4. Write the words that fit the boxes.

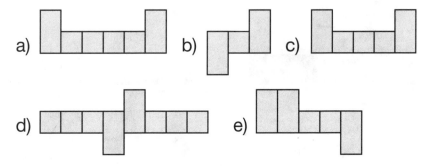

a)

b)

c)

d)

e)

Word Power

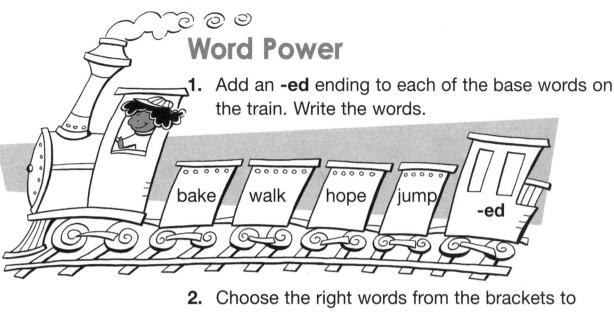

1. Add an **-ed** ending to each of the base words on the train. Write the words.

bake   walk   hope   jump   -ed

2. Choose the right words from the brackets to complete the sentences.

a) Yesterday I (play, played, playing) _____ ball.

b) We (looks, looking, looked) _____ everywhere.

c) They are (lived, living, lives) _____ on a farm.

3. Fill in the blanks with the correct contraction. Write each sentence.

it's   I'm

let's

can't   that's

don't

a) L_____ go to the store.

b) No, we c_____ because we d_____ have money.

c) T_____ too bad. I_____ almost lunch time and I_____ hungry.

4. Use words from the balloons to write about a parade you have seen, or would like to see.

band   float   march   clowns   airplane   truck

SUPER
★ ★ ★ ★ ★
nothing
friendly
stayed
puzzle
skated
★ ★ ★ ★ ★
WORDS

Challenges with Words

1. Complete the sentences with Super Words.
Write the sentences in your notebook.

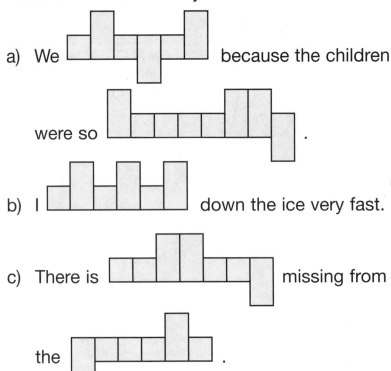

a) We [   ] because the children

were so [   ].

b) I [   ] down the ice very fast.

c) There is [   ] missing from

the [   ].

2. The word **friendly** has been written on pieces of a jigsaw puzzle. Combine the puzzle pieces in different ways. Make as many smaller words as you can.

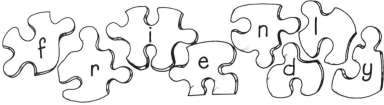

3. Find a Super Word that goes with the other two words. Write the word.

a) game   riddle   _____
b) happy   cheerful   _____
c) came   went   _____
d) everything   something   _____

120

Hint! The last letter of one word is the first letter of the next.

4. Find the words on the skater's path that end in **-ed**, **-ing**, and **-s**. Write them in your notebook.

Start here.

(skater's path words) gatheredigginggrabslippeddroppedallopeddrawsingrowdecidedwowskatedspinningdivingspinningallopeddrawsingrowdecidedwowskatedspinningdivingetslippingallopeddraw

5. Write about a winter day when your friends invite you to go skating. Use as many Super Words as you can. You may also want to use these words.

ice   slippery   laces   fell   bump

6. Here are some words for making pictures. Unscramble the words to complete these sentences.

a) I **denitap** a picture of my class.

b) My little brother **loocdure**.

c) I will **wdra** a picture for you, too!

26

Question Words
who

List Words

named
over
liked
mad
could
very
would
into
why
who
what

See the Words

1. Look carefully at the list words.

2. Look at the words. Notice the beginning letters.

   why   what   who

   What letters do many question words begin with?

Say the Words

Listen for each sound in the words as you say them.

could   would   named   liked   why   what

who   coming   very   mad   over

✓ Precheck

**Check your work.
Write the words
you misspelled.**

★ Powerbooster ★

Many question words begin with the letters **wh**.

who, what, when, where, why, which, whose

Write the Words

1. a) Read the letter that Mark wrote to his new pen pal.

> Dear Derek,
>
> I am <u>very</u> glad you are my new pen pal. First I will tell you <u>who</u> I am. My name is Mark and I have a brother <u>named</u> Steven. I <u>liked</u> your letter very much.
>
> <u>What</u> are you doing <u>over</u> the summer holidays? It <u>would</u> be great if you <u>could</u> visit us! <u>Why</u> don't you ask your parents?
>
> My parents will <u>get</u> <u>mad</u> if I don't go and help with the dishes right now, so I will put this letter <u>into</u> the mailbox.
>
> Your pen pal,
> Mark

b) Look for the list words in the letter. Write them in your notebook.

2. Write the three list words that are used to ask questions.

3. Write the base words for **liked** and **named**.

4. Write the two list words that rhyme.

5. Write the list words that fit the boxes.

a) 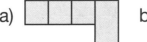 b)  c)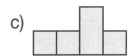

Word Power

1. Look at these pictures carefully. Write the missing word in each question below.

a) _____ is in the playpen?

b) _____ is the baby crying?

c) _____ does Nick's brother do?

d) _____ is Nick's teddy bear?

2. Add an **-ed** ending to each base word on the target. Write the words.

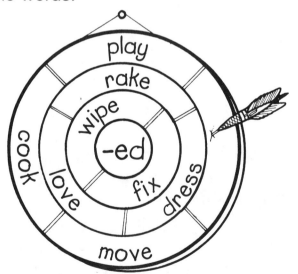

play
rake
wipe
-ed
fix
dress
move
love
cook

3. A good detective asks many questions. Write three questions about your class. Use one of these question words at the beginning of each sentence.

what   why   who

124

SUPER WORDS

surprised
excited
which
whose
ready

Challenges with Words

1. Fill in the blanks with Super Words using the clues below. Write the Super Words.

   a) This Super Word has the short **e** sound as in **let** and long **e** as in **me**. _____

   b) This Super Word has two **r**'s. _____

   c) These two Super Words are used to ask questions. _____ _____

   d) These two words drop the **e** when **-ed** is added. _____ _____

2. Complete the sentences with **who's** or **whose**. Write the sentences.

   a) _____ that boy with the brown cap?

   b) _____ dog is this?

   c) I don't know _____ at the door.

   d) She doesn't know _____ bike this is.

3. Use the endings **-ed** and **-ing** to make new words. Write the words.

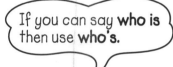

If you can say **who is** then use **who's**.

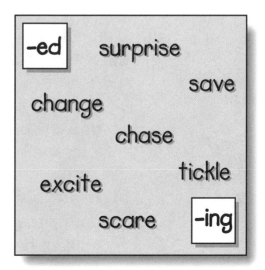

-ed surprise
            save
change
      chase
            tickle
excite
   scare -ing

4. These children are ready to go home, but they can't find their shoes!
Look at the picture. Write questions they might ask.

Where _____ ?
Which _____ ?
Whose _____ ?
What _____ ?

5. Write as many small words as you can using the letters of the word **surprised**.

6. a) Write about a time when you were surprised or excited. Don't forget to use the exclamation mark!

b) Read your story to a partner. Does your partner have any ideas about how you can make it better?

27

Vowel Sound

ow

n**ow**

school
children
how
after
now
teacher
love
happy
brown
town
catch

See the Words

Look at each list word carefully.

Say the Words

1. Say the words. Listen for each sound.

    how   town   brown   now   children

    teacher   catch   after   happy

    love   school

2. Say the words. Listen for the vowel sounds.

    now   town   how   brown

    What letters spell the vowel sound **ow** as in **now**?

3. Say the words. Listen for the **ch** sound as in **child**.

    children   teacher   catch

☑ Precheck

**Check your work.
Underline the
parts of the words
you need to study.**

★ Powerbooster ★

The vowel sound **ow** as in **clown** and **how** is
often spelled **ow**.

Write the Words

1. a) Read this story.

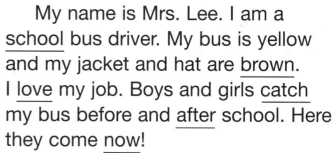

My name is Mrs. Lee. I am a <u>school</u> bus driver. My bus is yellow and my jacket and hat are <u>brown</u>. I <u>love</u> my job. Boys and girls <u>catch</u> my bus before and <u>after</u> school. Here they come <u>now</u>!

"Hello, Mrs. Lee," says the <u>teacher</u>. "<u>How</u> are you today?"

When all the <u>children</u> are on the bus, I drive around <u>town</u> until they are all safe and <u>happy</u> at home.

b) Look for the list words in the story. Write them in your notebook.

Here is a question word that **doesn't** start with **wh**!

2. Write the list words that rhyme with these picture words.

a)  b)

3. Write the list word that can be used to ask questions.

4. Write the list words that match these pictures.

 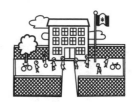

5. Write the four list words that have two syllables.

Remember, words that rhyme don't always look the same.

Word Power

1. Write as many words as you can that rhyme with the list words below.

school   now   town

2. Complete these sentences using the picture clues. Write the sentences.

a) The [girl] [boy] love **2** go to [school].

b) R U [smiley] now?

c) [can] U [catch] a [ball]?

3. Change the first letter of the word **catch** to make new words. Write the words.

Example   x̶catch   batch

catch | p | m | b | h |

4. a) Write a story using these list words.

school   teacher   children   happy

b) Make a poster that tells about your story.

129

SUPER
★ ★ ★ ★ ★
owl
shower
heart
change
chalk
★ ★ ★ ★ ★
WORDS

Challenges with Words

1. Use the following clues to write Super Words.

    a) two words with the sound **ow** as in **how**
    b) two words beginning with the **ch** sound as in **child**
    c) a word with a silent **l**
    d) a word meaning a part of the body

2. You need **chalk** in school. Make a list of other things that every school should have.

School Supplies	
Classroom	Playground
chalk	balls

3. Complete each set of words with a Super Word.

    a) rain   spring   _____
    b) brain   lung   _____
    c) pen   pencil   _____
    d) robin   crow   _____

4. Write smaller words using the letters in **heart**.

I found eleven words. See how many you can find.

heart

5. Complete each sentence. Write it in your notebook. Think carefully about your answers.

   a) A shower is like a bath because _____ .
      A shower is different than a bath because

      _____ .

   b) An owl is like a crow because _____ .
      An owl is different than a crow because

      _____ .

6. Add letters to the word **owl** to write new words. Use the clues below.

   a) what dogs do when they are angry _____
   b) what dogs do when they are lonely or sad

      _____
   c) another word for birds _____
   d) a word that means to go slowly and secretly

      _____

7. An owl is known for its wise sayings. Write what you think a wise owl would say about these things. Use **always** or **never** in your sentences.

   a) crossing the road
   b) brushing your teeth
   c) talking with strangers
   d) swimming in a pool

8. Here are some words you say when you feel excited. Write the words that fit the shapes. Complete each sentence with your own words.

   a) ▢▢▢ ! Look at that _____.

   b) ▢▢▢ ! Where are you _____?

   c) ▢▢ ! How are _____?

28

Consonant Sound **s**

ce

ni**ce**

elephant
rabbit
nice
place
bunny
lion
all
ball
rice
down
bear

See the Words

Look at each list word carefully.

Say the Words

1. Say the words and listen to each sound.

nice   place   all   ball   elephant   down

bear   bunny   lion   rabbit   rice

2. Say the words. Listen for the **s** sound at the end.

place   nice   rice

What letters spell the **s** sound at the end of the words?

✓ Precheck

Check your work. Write the words you misspelled.

★ Powerbooster ★

When we say **s** at the end of a word, we sometimes spell it **ce**.

Write the Words

1. a) Read the story Danny wrote.

> Last week our class took a trip down to the zoo. It was such a nice place to visit. I saw an elephant, a bear, a lion, a bunny rabbit, and lots of other animals. There was even a seal who played with a ball. We all had so much fun.

b) Look for the list words in the story. Write them in your notebook.

> **Syllables** are the number of parts you hear when you say a word. Each syllable has a vowel sound.

c) Write the list word that is not in the story. r_c_

2. Write the list words that have two syllables.

3. Write the word that has three syllables. Circle the two letters that make the **f** sound.

4. Write the three words that have the **s** sound at the end.

5. Complete the sentences with list words.

a) We [   ][   ] chased the  .

b) The  ran [ ][ ][ ] the hill.

133

Word Power

1. Write these animal words in alphabetical order.

   elephant   bear   rabbit   lion

2. Use the letters in the box to write words that end in **all**.

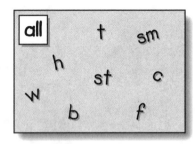

3. Complete these sentences.
   Write them in your notebook.

   a) A <u>r a</u> _ _ <u>i t</u> is sometimes called a
      <u>b u</u> _ _ <u>y</u>.
   b) The <u>e l e</u> _ _ _ <u>n t</u> and <u>l</u> _ _ <u>n</u>
      lived in the zoo.
   c) We had <u>r</u> _ _ <u>e</u> for dinner.

4. a) Complete the chart using the names of the
      animals in the box or your own ideas.

puppy	goldfish
sheep	elephant
lion	rabbit
kitten	bear
horse	tiger
goat	

Farm Animals	
House Pets	
Zoo Animals	

   b) Write a sentence that tells how farm animals
      are different than pets.

   Farm animals are different from pets
   because _____
   _____.

134

SUPER
★ ★ ★ ★ ★
downstairs
mice
space
shoelace
chance
★ ★ ★ ★ ★
WORDS

Challenges with Words

1. Complete the sentences using Super Words.

   a) My _____ broke on the way to school.
   b) There is no air in outer _____ .
   c) We found our pet _____ when we went
      _____ .
   d) Take a _____ ! You might win a prize.

2. Write the Super Words that match these clues.

   a) four words that have the **s** sound spelled **ce**
   b) a word with the **ow** sound as in **now** spelled **ow**
   c) two compound words
   d) two words with the long **a** sound as in **face**

3. Make words with the word wheels. Write the
   words in your notebook.

a)
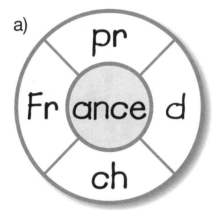

b)
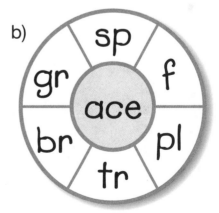

Divide into teams. See whose stairs are the longest.

4. Play the game 'Going Downstairs'. Write a four-letter word going across. Then write a four-letter word going down. Make stairs until you run out of words.

Here are some examples.

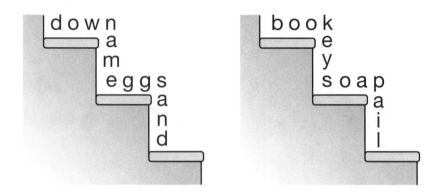

```
d o w n
      a
      m
      e g g s
          a
          n
          d
```

```
b o o k
      e
      y
      s o a p
          a
          i
          l
```

5. a) Write about where you might like to go on a trip to outer space. Use the sentence starter below to help.

> I would like to go to _____
> _____ .

b) Make a list of things you might see on your trip. Work with a partner.

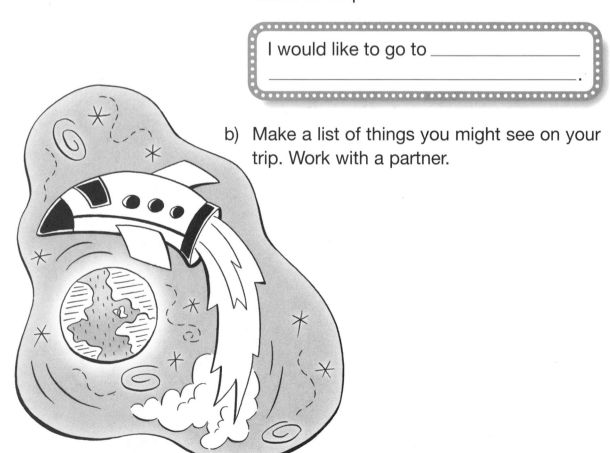

family
flowers
find
little
kitten
things
spring
letter
dance
pretty
animals

See the Words

Look at the shape of each word.

Say the Words

1. Listen for each sound as you say the words.

   find   things   spring   dance   flowers   little

   kitten   letter   pretty   family   animals

2. Say the words. Listen for how many parts are in each word.

   flowers   little   kitten   letter   pretty

   family   animals

   We call each word part a **syllable**. Say each word again. How many vowel sounds do you hear in each **syllable**?

★ Powerbooster ★

Many words can be broken up into parts called **syllables**. Every **syllable** has a vowel sound as in **fam i ly**.

Write the Words

1. a) Read this letter that Gina wrote.

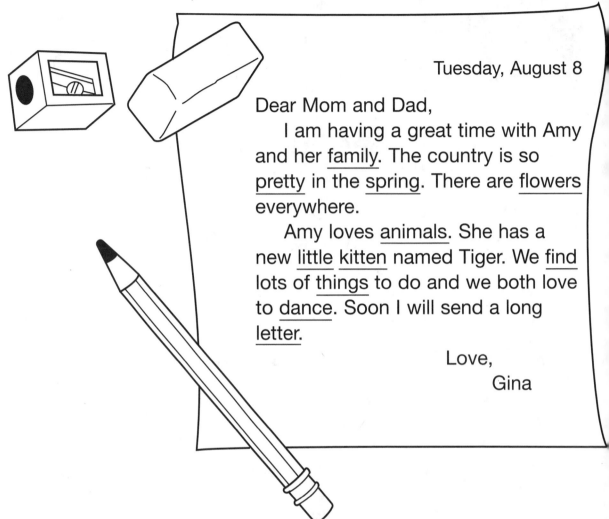

Tuesday, August 8

Dear Mom and Dad,
    I am having a great time with Amy and her <u>family</u>. The country is so <u>pretty</u> in the <u>spring</u>. There are <u>flowers</u> everywhere.
    Amy loves <u>animals</u>. She has a new <u>little</u> <u>kitten</u> named Tiger. We <u>find</u> lots of <u>things</u> to do and we both love to <u>dance</u>. Soon I will send a long <u>letter</u>.

Love,
Gina

b) Look for all the list words in the letter.
    Write them in your notebook.

2. Write the five list words that have two syllables.

3. Write the two list words that have three syllables.

4. Write the list word that uses the letters **ce** to spell the **s** sound.

5. Write the two list words that have the letters **-ing**.

138

Word Power

1. Copy each word below. Write the number of syllables you hear when you say each word.

    Example   butter 2

    apple   potato   milk
    sugar   pancake   banana

2. Write the picture words. They all rhyme with **spring**.

3. Solve these riddles. The answers are list words.

    a) I am playful.   b) To write me is fun.
        I lost my mitten.   To get me is better.
        Can you guess?   I have a stamp.
        I am a _____ .   I am a _____ .

4. Write a letter to a new pen pal. Tell your pen pal the things you like to do with the people in your family. You might want to start your letter like this.

    _____ , _____ __

    Dear _____

      My name is _____ .

    There are _____ people
    in my _____ .

SUPER
★ ★ ★ ★ ★
weather
rainbow
fruit
robin
umbrella
★ ★ ★ ★ ★
WORDS

Challenges with Words

1. Complete the sentences with Super Words.
Write the words in your notebook.

    a) After a spring shower we sometimes see
a _ _ _ _ _ _ _ .

    b) I love to walk in the rain with my
_ _ _ _ _ _ _ _ .

    c) When the w_ _ther gets warmer, the
r_ _ _ _s fly north.

2. Solve these riddles. The answers are Super
Words. Write the words.

Sometimes I'm sweet,	I have many colours,
Sometimes I'm sour,	Do you wonder why?
But I always begin	When the rain is over,
As a blossom or flower.	I decorate the sky!
I am _____ .	I am a _____ .

3. Write each Super Word. Beside it write the
number of syllables you hear.

4. Write sentences about the children in the pictures. You may want to use these weather words.

sunny   cloudy   raining   snowing

windy   umbrella   rainbow   weather

5. Here are two words with three syllables and lots of **a**'s!

a) We live in __ a __ a __ a.

b) I love to eat a __ a __ a __ a.

c) The tennis player wore a blue b__ __ d__ __ a.

30

Looking Back

Here is a list of words from Units 25–29 that may be hard for you.

could	family	children	lived
teacher	pretty	can't	very
school	coming	let's	flowers

look

say

cover

write

check

1. Study the words using the five Study Steps. Add some words of your own to the review list.

2. Write the review word that goes with each clue.

   a) someone who teaches
   b) a place to learn
   c) the opposite of ugly
   d) the opposite of going
   e) more than one child
   f) the people you live with

3. Write the question word you would use in these sentences. Use the words in the box.

How	When	Where	Who	What

   a) _____ does school start?
   b) _____ did you put my letter?
   c) _____ will play with me?
   d) _____ will you do on Saturday?
   e) _____ many people are in your family?

Watch for words that drop an **e**!

4. Add an **-ed** ending to each base word on the wheel. Write the words.

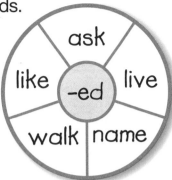

ask
like   -ed   live
walk   name

5. Write contractions for the underlined words in each sentence.

a) I <u>can not</u> go with you.
b) <u>I am</u> sorry you are sick.
c) <u>Let us</u> play in the park.
d) <u>Do not</u> forget your pencil.

6. Write the words that have the same sound as these letters.

a) **y** in **baby**

   my   bunny   very   why   pretty   happy

b) **c** in **mice**

   cup   nice   place   truck   dance   sing

c) **a** in **cake**

   named   rabbit   place   played   can't

d) **ow** in **flowers**

   school   town   now   low   tow   how

7. a) Make new words by adding letters to **ice** and **ace**. Write the words in your notebook.

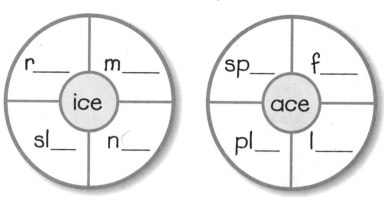

b) Choose three words you have made. Write a sentence with each word.

8. Write the animal names from the word box that match these clues.

Animals
kangaroo
shark
dinosaur
tiger
groundhog
mouse
butterfly
whale
rabbit

a) animal names with one syllable

_____ _____ _____

b) animal names with two syllables

_____ _____ _____

c) animal names with three syllables

_____ _____ _____

9. Make your own review list with words from your writing, Super Words, or words from the Unit Tests. Don't forget the five Study Steps.

Find a partner to dictate your list to you.

Transportation

airplane

wings

COME TO THE CIRCUS!

train

engine

caboose

track

truck

wheels

1. The circus is coming. Look at the picture. Write all the words that tell about moving the circus from one place to another.

2. Make three headings in your notebook.

train
ship   canoe
helicopter   sailboat
jet   bicycle   bus
car   airplane

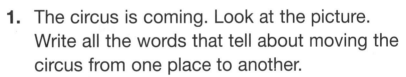

Land Travel	Water Travel	Air Travel

Write the words in the balloon under the correct heading.

3. Write a report about the ways you and people in your family go from place to place.

Grammar Games

Joining Words

There are two small words we use to join sentences,
and and **but**.

I like dogs. I like cats.
I like dogs **and** cats.

I like dogs. I don't like cats.
I like dogs, **but** I don't
like cats.

1. Use **and** to join these sentences.

    a) I have cake. I have balloons.
    b) She likes hot dogs. She likes mustard.
    c) We love toys. We love games.

2. Use **and** or **but** to complete these sentences.
    Write the sentences in your notebook.

    a) I like bananas _____ oranges.
    b) I like apples, _____ I hate pineapple.
    c) I go to school on Friday, _____ I don't
        go on Saturday.

145a

Dictionary Games

1. a) Write the words you find in the picture that begin with **q**, **r**, **s**, **t**, and **u**.

q _____ _____ _____

r _____ _____ _____ _____

s _____ _____ _____ _____

t _____ _____ _____ _____

u _____ _____

b) Write sentences using some of the words you found for each of the letters above.

145b

31

Long **i**

igh

n**igh**t

See the Words

Look at each word in the list.

Say the Words

1. Say each word. Listen for each sound.

night   might   water   watch   want

really   people   bird   grass   summer   long

2. Say the words. Listen for the vowel sounds.

night   might   sight   light

What letters spell the long **i** sound as in **ice**?

grass
summer
long
water
watch
want
night
might
really
people
bird

✓ Precheck

Check your work. What words do you need to study?

★ Powerbooster ★

Sometimes we use the letters **igh** to spell the long **i** sound as in **ice**.

☀ Write the Words

1. a) Read this story.

I really like summer. I like to walk barefoot in the long grass. I like to watch the bird that makes its nest under my window. I like to play in the water and see all the people at the beach. This year I might be able to swim across the river.

There's only one thing I don't like about summer. When the days are long, I don't want to go to bed at night!

b) Look for the list words in the story.
Write them in your notebook.

2. Write the two list words that rhyme with **light**. Underline the letters that make the long **i** sound as in **ice**.

3. Write the list words that have two syllables.

4. Write the list words that fit the boxes.

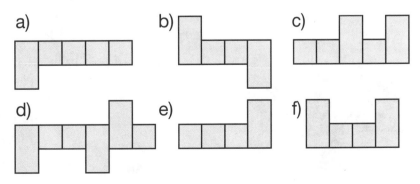

a)   b)   c)

d)   e)   f)

Word Power

1. Write words that rhyme with **might**.
The clues will help you.

    a) the opposite of day   ____ ight
    b) the opposite of dull   ____ ight
    c) the opposite of dark   ____ ight
    d) the opposite of loose   ____ ight
    e) the opposite of left   ____ ight

2. Write the words that complete this story.

The su_ _er holidays will soon be here. I like

to walk in the ＿＿＿＿＿ and

the ＿＿＿＿ in the ＿＿＿＿ .

When it is r_ _ _ _ly hot, I

in the ＿＿＿＿＿ .

3. a) What will you do when summer comes?
Make a list of things you hope to do. Use list
words if you can. Share your list with a
friend.

    b) Make a booklet showing your summer
activities. Fold a piece of paper like this.

Make a picture for each section.

SUPER
★ ★ ★ ★ ★
nighttime
moonlight
waterfall
autumn
sight
★ ★ ★ ★ ★
WORDS

Challenges with Words

1. Write the three Super Words that are compounds. Put a box around the two small words in each compound.

2. Write the word that means the same as **fall**. Circle the silent letter.

3. Solve these riddles with Super Words. Write the words.

   a) The days are shorter
       The nights are cooler
       Leaves begin to fall
       It must be _____ .

   b) The sun goes down
       The moon comes out
       It is time for bed
       It must be _____ .

   c) Loud noises
       Lots of spray
       Water tumbling down
       We must be near a _____ .

4. Write your own riddles for the other two Super Words. Share them with a partner.

5. Find the Super Words that fit the boxes. Write the words.

I love writing riddles.

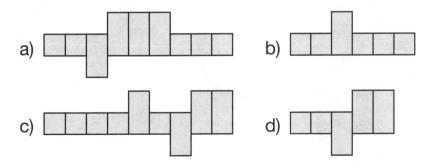

a)   b)

c)   d)

6. Make words with the word wheels. What do you notice about the sound of **ite** and **ight**?

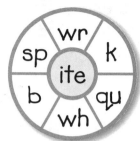

7. Complete these sentences with words from exercise 6. Write the sentences in your notebook.

a) That dog will __ite! It gave me a bad __ __ight.

b) Niagara Falls is __ __ite a __ight.

c) The sun on the __ __ite snow is very __ __ight.

d) The __ __ight of a __ite is like a big bird.

8. Use some of your **ite** and **ight** words to write a poem.

9. Here are some words you can use to talk about clothes. Write the words that fit each shape.

a) My jacket is [   ] green.

b) His shoes were too [   ] .

c) This is a [   ] sweater.

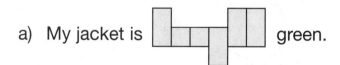

150

32

Long **e**   Long **o**
y   **ow**
pupp**y**   gr**ow**

mommy
glad
milk
daddy
store
puppy
know
food
pony
grow .
cute

See the Words

Look at each word in the list.

Say the Words

1. Listen for each sound as you say the words.

mommy   daddy   puppy   pony   grow
know   cute   glad   food   store   milk

2. Say the words. Listen for the final vowel sound.
mommy   daddy   puppy   pony
What letter spells the long **e** sound as in **puppy**?

3. Say the words. Listen for the vowel sound.
grow   tow   crow
What letters spell the long **o** sound as in **grow**?

✓ Precheck

**Check your work.
Write the words
you misspelled.**

★ Powerbooster ★

We often use the letter **y** to spell the long **e** sound
at the end of a word with two syllables, as in **puppy**.

Sometimes we use the letters **ow** to spell the
long **o** sound as in **grow**.

Write the Words

1. a) Read this story.

My family owns a corner store. We sell milk, bread, and other things that we know people often need. My mommy and daddy work very hard in the store. I am busy too. I look after our cute puppy named Wiggles. Right now he is small, but soon he will grow as big as a pony. I'm glad we also have lots of dog food in our store! Wiggles will need it.

b) Look for all the list words in the story. Write them in your notebook.

2. Write the list words that rhyme with **bow**. Underline the letters that spell the long **o** sound as in **grow**.

3. Write the list words that end with the long **e** sound as in **baby**.

4. Write the list words that fit the boxes.

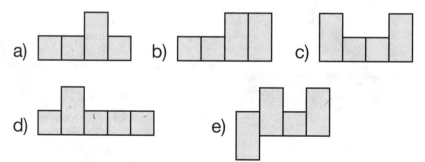

a)   b)   c)

d)   e)

5. Write the list word that has a silent **k**.

Remember **ow** can also say **ow** as in **now**.

Word Power

1. Add each consonant blend to **ow** to make new words. Write the words.

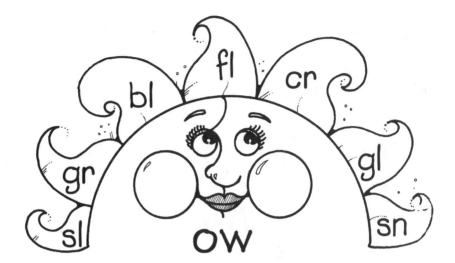

2. Write each picture word. They all end in the letter **y**.

a)   b)   c)   d)

3. Complete each sentence with a word from the box. Write the sentences in your notebook.

a) Smile if you are _____.

b) We are _____ it didn't rain.

c) The flowers look very _____ .

d) The clown was so _____ .

pretty
funny
lucky
happy

4. Write about how your family gets its food. Use as many list words as you can. You might need some of the words in the box.

| supermarket | shopping cart | buy |

153

Challenges with Words

1. Write the two Super Words that have silent consonants. Underline the silent letters.

2. Unscramble the words on the lamb. They are all Super Words. Write the words.

a) nefik

b) rogcyre

c) mabl

d) trhow

e) ketarm

a) _____

b) _____

c) _____

d) _____

e) _____

3. Fill in the blanks with Super Words. These sentences are both from nursery rhymes.

a) This little pig went to _____ .

b) Mary had a little _____ .

4. Complete the sentences with Super Words. Write the sentences.

a) We buy food at the ☐☐☐☐☐☐

store and the ☐☐☐☐☐ .

b) Tom cut the bread with a sharp ☐☐☐☐ .

c) The ☐☐☐☐ ran after the sheep.

154

5. Make more words that end in **mb** using the word wheel. Write the words.

6. Read the nursery rhyme.

Mary had a little lamb,
Its fleece was white as snow.
And everywhere that Mary went,
The lamb was sure to go.

It followed her to school one day,
Which was against the rule.
It made the children laugh and play,
To see a lamb at school!

a) Write a short story about what the lamb did when it followed Mary to school.

b) Draw a picture to go with your story.

7. a) What would happen if a pet followed you to school? Share some ideas with a partner.

b) Write a story or poem about an animal that visits your school.

33

Long e
ey
monkey

bears
caught
rabbits
elephants
horse
birds
oh
goes
door
monkey
years
hockey

✓ Precheck

Check your work. Underline the parts of the words you need to study.

See the Words

Look at each word in the list.

Say the Words

1. Say each word. Listen for each sound.

   bears   birds   elephants   rabbits   years

   oh   goes   caught   horse   door   hockey

   monkey

2. Say the words. Listen for the final vowel sound.

   monkey   turkey   hockey

What letters spell the long **e** sound as in **me**?

★ Powerbooster ★

In some words the long **e** sound is spelled **ey**, as in **monkey** and **donkey**.

156

Write the Words

1. a) Read this story.

Mark always <u>goes</u> to his favourite toy store with his <u>little</u> brother Steven. Mark likes the <u>hockey</u> games and model kits at the back of the store. But Steven is only four <u>years</u> old. He likes the stuffed toys just inside the <u>door</u>.

One day they went to the store. Steven called, "Come and see all the teddy <u>bears</u>, the <u>rabbits</u> and the <u>birds</u>, and the <u>elephants</u>. Come and see the rocking <u>horse</u>!" Just then a toy <u>monkey</u> <u>caught</u> his eye. "<u>Oh</u>," said Steven, "that's the best toy of all."

b) Look for all the list words in the story. Write them in your notebook.

Remember! Words that mean **more than one** are called plurals.

2. Write the two list words that have the long **e** sound spelled **ey** as in **key**.

3. Write the five list words that mean **more than one**.

4. Write the two list words with the sound **or** as in **order**.

5. Write the words that fit these boxes.

a) 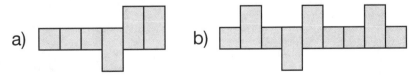 b)

c)

Word Power

1. Complete the sentences with list words. Write them in your notebook.

   a) These <u>b</u> _ _ <u>d s</u> are two <u>y</u> _ _ <u>r s</u> old.

   b) _ <u>h</u>! there <u>g</u> _ _ <u>s</u> the <u>h o</u> _ _ _ <u>y</u> team!

   c) The police <u>c</u> _ _ _ _ <u>t</u> the robbers at the <u>d</u> _ _ <u>r</u>.

2. Write two list words that have the short **o** sound as in **hot**. Write the words. Circle the letters that spell the short **o**.

3. Write the picture words.

   a)    b) 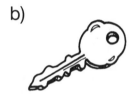   c)

4. Complete each set of words with a list word.

a)	puck	net	_____
b)	enter	exit	_____
c)	rider	saddle	_____
d)	long ears	short tails	_____

5. a) Write sentences with these word pairs.

   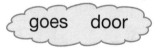

   goes   door   elephants   bears

   b) Read your sentences with a partner.

*Hint! One of the words rhymes with **thought**!*

158

SUPER
⋆ ⋆ ⋆ ⋆ ⋆
zebra
turkey
birdhouse
fear
camel
⋆ ⋆ ⋆ ⋆ ⋆
WORDS

Challenges with Words

1. Solve these riddles. The answers are all Super Words. Write them in your notebook.

a) I have humps on my back
   and I live in the desert.
   I am a _____ .

b) I'm a key
   that starts with t.
   I am a _____ .

c) I look like a horse
   but I'm black and white.
   I am a _____ .

2. Complete these sentences. Write your answers in your notebook.

a) A zebra is like a horse because _____ .

   A zebra is different than a horse because _____ .

b) A turkey is like a robin because _____ .

   A turkey is different than a robin because _____ .

c) A birdhouse is like a doghouse because _____ .

   A birdhouse is different than a doghouse because _____ .

3. a) Unscramble the letters on each birdhouse to make a Super Word.

b) Use each word to write a sentence.

4. Make two short sentences into one long sentence. Write the sentences.

a) We saw a zebra at the zoo. We saw a camel at the zoo.

b) Eagles are large birds. Turkeys are large birds.

5. Use the picture clues to write words ending in **key**.

6. Change the first letter of **fear** to make new words. Use these letters.

g   t   h   n   sp   cl

7. Here are some more interesting animal names. Write the names that fit the sentences.

a) A blue _ _ _ _ _ is the largest animal.

b) A _ _ _ _ _ _ _ _ _ _ _ _ _ _ _ loves mud and lives in a river.

c) An _ _ _ _ _ _ _ _ _ _ is an animal with lots of teeth and a long tail.

Kids
WORDS

alligator
whale
hippopotamus

160

34

Vowel Sound **ow**

ou	**ow**
out	c**ow**

---

friends
our
story
once
about
out
never
together
old
told
horses
cow

✓ Precheck

**Check your work.
Write the words
you misspelled.**

See the Words

Look at each word in the list.

Say the Words

1. Listen to the sounds as you say each word.

   our out about cow old told once
   never together story horses friends

2. Say the words. Listen for the vowel sound.

   our   out   about

Write the Words

1. a) Read this story.

This is a true <u>story</u> <u>about</u> <u>our</u> horses, Brownie and Buck. <u>Once</u> they were in the field with our <u>old</u> <u>cow</u>, Patches. Patches made a hole in the fence and they all went down the road <u>together</u>. When they came to Mrs. Brown's garden, they stopped and began to eat. "Get <u>out</u>, get out!" Mrs. Brown <u>told</u> the three animals, but they just kept on eating. At last our <u>friends</u> came along in their truck. They brought our animals home, and we fixed the fence. They <u>never</u> got out again!

b) Look for the list words in the story.
Write them in your notebook.

2. Write the four list words with the vowel sound **ow**. Underline the letters that spell **ow**.

3. Write the two sets of rhyming words in the list.

4. Write the list word that has three syllables.

5. Write the list word that rhymes with **bends**.

6. Write the word **once**. Underline the letters that spell the sound **s**.

Word Power

1. Use the letters on the gold coins to write words that rhyme with **old**.

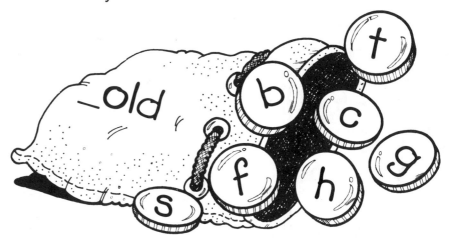

2. Complete these sentences with list words.

   a) Have you _o l d your f r _ _ _ n d s a b _ _ t _ _ r plans?

   b) Let's go there t o g _ _ _ e r.

   c) O n _ _ I let the h _ _ _ _ s _ _ t by mistake.

3. Make new words by adding letters to **out** and **ound**. Write the words.

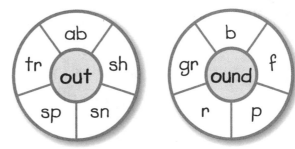

4. a) Write a **true** story about something that happened to you or your friends. Use as many list words as you can.

   b) Read your story out load to a small group.

SUPER
★ ★ ★ ★ ★
bounce
storybook
outfit
loud
sound
★ ★ ★ ★ ★
WORDS

Challenges with Words

1. Write the Super Words with the vowel sound **ow**.

2. Write the Super Words that are compounds. Put a box around each part of the compound.

3. Look at each picture. What is wrong with the outfits the children are wearing? Write a sentence for each picture.

4. Use the clues to write words that rhyme with **pound**.

   a) the shape of a circle
   b) what our ears hear
   c) the opposite of lost
   d) our feet walk on it
   e) a kind of dog

5. Complete the sentences with Super Words.
Write the sentences in your notebook.

a) Do not <u>b</u> <u>o</u> <u>u</u> <u>n</u> <u>c</u> <u>e</u> on the bed!

b) Please read me a _____ .

c) I would like to wear this _____ .

d) I love the <u>s</u> _ _ _ <u>d</u> of that _____ music.

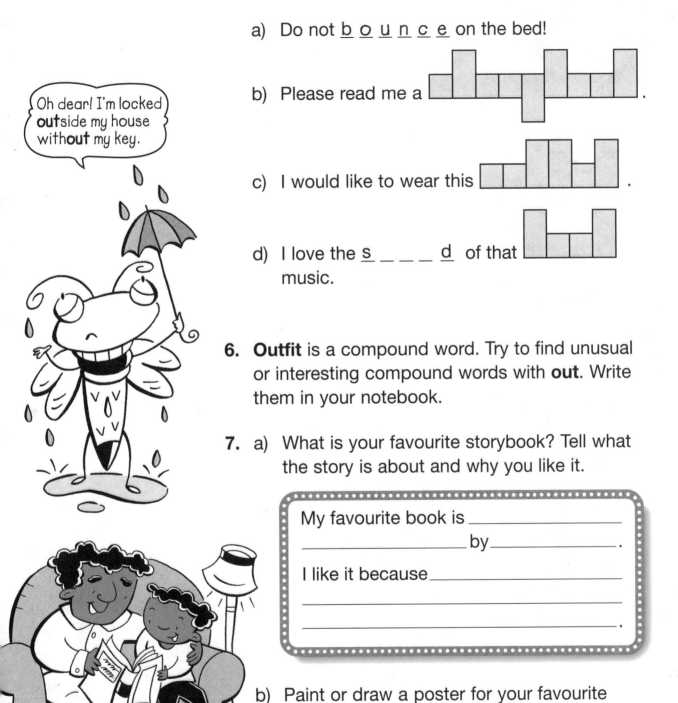

Oh dear! I'm locked **out**side my house with**out** my key.

6. Outfit is a compound word. Try to find unusual or interesting compound words with **out**. Write them in your notebook.

7. a) What is your favourite storybook? Tell what the story is about and why you like it.

My favourite book is _____
_____ by _____ .
I like it because _____
_____
_____ .

b) Paint or draw a poster for your favourite book.

Looking Back

35

STUDY STEPS

look

say

cover

write

check

Here are some words from Units 31–34 that may be hard for you.

really	friends	our	bears
people	once	might	summer
caught	together	watch	bird
elephants	animals	know	goes

1. Study the words using the five Study Steps. Add your own difficult words.

2. Look for words from the Review List that mean **more than one**. Change them to mean **just one**.

   Example   people – person

3. a) Write the picture words that mean **more than one**.

   b) What letter did you use at the end of each word?

4. Use the letters and pictures to write each word.

   mon   y   don

5. Write the words below in your notebook. Draw a circle around the words with two syllables. Underline the words with three syllables.

family   rabbits   elephant   horses

story   together   about

6. Write the picture words. They all end in the long **e** sound as in **me**.

Don't forget to use an apostrophe.

7. Write contractions for the underlined words.

a) <u>I am</u> sorry you <u>did not</u> see the circus.

b) I <u>can not</u> come because I <u>do not</u> know the way.

c) <u>It is</u> a great day. <u>Let us</u> go to the park.

d) <u>We are</u> going to the zoo.

e) <u>There is</u> a ball on the roof.

8. Make each word mean **more than one**. Write the words.

night   store   door   year   cow

teacher   school   truck   town   lion

9. Remember that there is more than one way to spell the vowel sound **ow** as in **owl**.
Make two headings in your notebook. Put the words in the box under the correct heading.

ou—**ow**	ou—**ou**

sour	mouth	crown
town	mouse	ground
round	brown	cow
now	loud	frown
house	how	bound

long **o**	long **e**
sh**ow**	happ**y**
_____	_____
_____	_____
_____	_____

10. Look in some of your favourite reading books.

a) Make a list of words that have the final long **o** sound as in **snow**.

b) Make another list of words that end with the long **e** sound written with a **y** as in **puppy**.

Now make your own review list.

11. Make your own review list. Use the five Study Steps to study your list. Now find a partner to dictate it to you.

Summer Holidays

lifeguard · Frisbee · bike · kite · lake · beach · pool · hide and seek · picnic · ball · hike

- go to the movies
- ride my bike
- play cards
- play in the sprinkler
- watch cartoons
- fly kites

1. Look at the picture. All the words are about things to do in the summer.

a) Make two columns in your notebook like this.

Inside	Outside

b) Write all the things you can do inside, in the summer, in one column. Write all the things you can do outside in the other. Use the picture to help you.

2. a) Write about some things you will remember about your class this year.

b) Put your stories together to make a class book. Add your photos and a sentence about each author.

Grammar Games

Question Mark

We put a **question mark** at the end of a sentence that asks a question.

What is your favourite colour**?**

Exclamation mark

We put an exclamation mark at the end of a sentence that shows surprise or anger.

Look out for the wet floor**!**

The word with the **capital** is the first word.

1. Put a question mark or exclamation mark at the end of these sentences. Write the sentences in your notebook.

   a) Where are you going __
   b) Watch my foot __
   c) What is your name __
   d) Please, help me __

2. Unscramble these sentences. Write them in the correct order.

   a) you How are ? old
   b) a ! bike What great
   c) do live Where ? you
   d) out ! Watch the car for

Dictionary Games

welcome

Welcome to the ZOO

zoo

zebra

van

yard

yak

wave

water

vest

x-ray

vet

1. Find words in the picture that begin with the letters **v**, **w**, **x**, **y**, and **z**.

v _____   _____   _____

w _____   _____   _____

x _____

y _____   _____

z _____   _____

169b

Basic Word List

Many of these words are in the list of the 200 most
frequently misspelled words. The words with an * beside
them are in the top 25 most frequently misspelled words.

a	black	Dad	for
about	blue	daddy	found
after	book	dance	friend *
airplane	box	day	friends *
all	boy	did	from
am	boys	didn't *	fun
an	brother	do	funny
and	brown	dog	
animals	bunny	dogs	gave
are	bus	doll	get
as	but	don't	girl
asked	by	door	girls
at		down	give
ate	cake		glad
away	came	eat	go
	can	elephant	goes
baby	can't	elephants	going
back	car		good
bad	cat	family	got
ball	catch	farm	grass
be	cats	fast	green
bear	caught *	father	grow
bears	children	feed	
because *	come	fell	had
bed	comes	find	happy
bee	coming	fish	has
big	could	fishing	have
bird	cow	five	hay
birds	cup	flowers	he
birthday	cute	food	help

her
him
his
hit
hockey
home
hope
horse
horses
hot
house
how

I
if
I'm
in
into *
is
it
it's *

jet
jump
just

kitten
know

let
let's *
letter
like
liked
likes
lion
little
live

lived
long
look
looked
lost
lot
lots
love

mad
made
make
makes
man
may
me
might
milk
Mom
mommy
monkey
morning
mother
mouse
my

name
named
never
new
next
nice
night
nine
no
not
now

of
off *
oh
old
on
once
one
or
other
our
out
outside
over

park
people
pet
pets
pig
pigs
place
play
played
playing
plays
pony
pretty
puppy
put

rabbit
rabbits
ran
read
really
red
rice
ride

riding
run

sad
said *
saw
say
school
see
seven
she
sister
six
sleep
so
some
something *
sometimes
spring
start
store
story
summer
sun
swim
swimming

take
teacher
that
that's *
the
their *
them
then
there *
they *
thing

things
this
three
time
to
today
together
told
too
took
town
tree
trees
truck
try
two

up
upon *
us

very

walk
walking
want
was
watch
water
way
we
went *
were *
what
when *
where *
white
who

why
will
wish
with
work
would

years
yes
yesterday
you
your